Joysticks, BLINKING LIGHTS, and Thrills

How to Have Fun and Success in Your Business

Joseph M. Sherlock

OASIS PRESS BOOKS & SOFTWARE

The Oasis Press® /PSI Research
Grants Pass, Oregon
042597

Published by The Oasis Press®/PSI Research
© 1997 by Joseph M. Sherlock

This publication is designed to provide accurate and authoritative information in regard to the subject matter covered. It is sold with the understanding that the author and publisher are not engaged in rendering legal, accounting, or other professional service. If legal advice or other expert assistance is required, the services of a competent professional person should be sought.

> *— from a declaration of principles jointly adopted by a
> committee of the American Bar Association and a committee of publishers.*

Editor: Karen Billipp
Interior design by Eliot House Productions
Cover illustration and design by Steven Burns

Please direct any comments, questions, or suggestions regarding this book to
The Oasis Press®/PSI Research:

Editorial Department
300 North Valley Drive
Grants Pass, OR 97526
(541) 479-9464
(541) 476-1479 *fax*
psi2@magick.net *email*

The Oasis Press® is a Registered Trademark of Publishing Services, Inc., an Oregon corporation doing business as PSI Research.

Library of Congress Cataloging-in-Publication Data

Sherlock, Joseph M., 1943–
   Joysticks, blinking lights & thrills : how to have fun & success in your small business / Joseph M. Sherlock.
      p.   cm.
     Includes bibliographical references and index.
     ISBN 1-55571-401-3 (pbk.)
      1. Small business—Management.   I. Title.
HD62.7.S526 1997   97-1313
658.02'2—dc21   CIP

Printed in the United States of America
First Edition 10 9 8 7 6 5 4 3 2 1 0

✇ Printed on recycled paper when available

Table of Contents

Acknowledgments

This book may have my name on it but there have many people involved in its making.

First, I'd like to thank John M. Koegler. John was my partner in our plastics manufacturing business. Together we learned a lot about what makes a small business work and not work. John has always been a source of valuable ideas and advice. He now owns a wood furniture manufacturing business, so every day John deals with many of the issues discussed in this book.

Dr. H. J. Gambino is the author of several books and articles on business management. He wrote the Foreword and critiqued many portions of this text. His sensible advice made this a better book and I'm grateful for his help. Don't let his Ph.D. fool you. Harry has owned and run several businesses including a manufacturing firm, an aircraft accessory mail order business, a hair and skin salon and an advertising consulting firm.

I'd also like to express my gratitude to Steve Poe, salesman extraordinaire, who reviewed the sections on selling and customer service. Thanks also to Jim Farrell, automobile enthusiast and historian, who reviewed the "Lessons From Detroit" chapter. Jim is a car expert who owns a perfect 1941 Lincoln Continental Cabriolet as well as some other wonderful and desirable old automobiles. My appreciation also extends to my publisher, Emmett Ramey of Oasis Press, who believed in this book, and Karen Billipp who skillfully edited it, making it a better and far more readable work. Special thanks to my clients who continue to give me further insights into the world of small business.

Finally, I'd like to thank my wife, my best friend, and love of my life, Carol. She stood by me during the tough times in my first business, providing emotional and financial support. Her advice and counsel during all of our years together have been invaluable to me. She is the sea of calm, smoothing out my tsunamis of impulsiveness. Because of Carol, I have lived the life I've always dreamed of. She also patiently proofread every page of my manuscript and gave me lots of suggestions about how to improve it.

Foreword

Been there! Done that! These four words perfectly describe Joe Sherlock's qualifications to write a book on small business management. In short, he's done it all. He has grown and prospered in the world of small business where many have gone and most have failed.

If experience is the best teacher, then Joe has certainly been well taught. His business career spans more than a quarter century and runs the complete gamut of business life. He started as a technical representative, then a market manager, for a major Fortune 200 company in Philadelphia, Pennsylvania, where he was responsible for the introduction and growth of a number of new product segments. He left that position to become a partner in a small plastics manufacturing and distribution company in Oregon.

The company started in a downtown Corvallis storefront with two full-time employees, Joe and his partner, John Koegler. Eleven years later, they had grown the business into a 38,000 square foot factory in an industrial park in the Corvallis suburbs, and had 73 full-time employees running three shifts. Then, at the height of their accomplishments, they did what many enterprising, innovative, and very successful entrepreneurs do. They sold the company to an even larger business and retired.

Retirement is no real option for a man with the energy and drive of a Joe Sherlock. So he started another business, Sherlock Strategies, a consulting firm that specializes in helping small businesses grow and prosper. As a consultant, Joe shares his experience gained from a lifetime in the business world, along with his innate talent for business, his common-sense approach to business, and his managerial acumen in a way that lets others achieve success.

Now, in book form, Joe has shared the business wisdom he has accumulated over the years, sharing the good moments with the bad. Each chapter is a sound lesson in small business management.

Don't just read this book. Study it. Devour it. Use it. Put into practice the lessons it preaches. This is not a book to be read and put on the shelf to gather dust. It is a book to live with and to live by.

Joe Sherlock has profited from his experience and knowledge. The lessons in this book will let you profit from that same experience and knowledge, as well.

— Henry J. Gambino, Ph.D.,
Aeone Communications,
Doylestown, PA

Introduction

This book is for entrepreneurs who have big dreams for their small business but limited time and financial resources. They must make their resources work extra hard to accomplish their goals. This book shows how to do just that. It provides practical and affordable ideas for making your business a stellar success.

In this book, you'll find stories about joysticks, blinking lights, thrills, gate-keepers, thugs, plastics, gold, silt, mud, Somat machines, Edsels, booger tape and lots of other things. They are all devices to help explain how to run a successful small business. Several analogies are also used throughout this book to describe the process of efficient small business operation.

Running a business is as easy as baking a cake. Well, it can be if you'll let it. Precious business hours are often wasted looking for mixing bowls and measuring cups because we're so disorganized. Or we spend our days tearing open the cupboards of business trivia searching for the right ingredients. We worry ceaselessly about whether our cake will turn out right. Then we get rushed and frustrated and don't take the time to mix the batter thoroughly or fail to let it bake long enough. Or, after doing a competent job of mixing and baking, we impatiently slather on the icing in a careless manner, ruining the presentation of our finished cake. Or we spend so much time in a tither and get so upset that, when our cake is finally ready to be served, we're so exhausted that we're unable to enjoy it. It's no fun.

Whether you own a business, manage a business or manage a segment of a business, it can be a piece of cake if you know the rules and follow a few simple steps. This book explores the key recipe elements and the proper preparation methods. Focus on them and you'll get great results from all your baking efforts. And you'll have fun, too.

Enjoy your cake!

How to Read
(and Mutilate) This Book

When running my own small plastics manufacturing business, I spent several days each month on the road. I often spent my evenings reading books about business. Wanting to learn how to make my small business better, I was always looking for new ideas. I read five to .10 business books each month. Over the course of a few years, I had read hundreds of business books and had gotten thousands of good ideas. I used these ideas to make my business more successful.

A few of the books I read weren't very good but they were almost never worthless. If a book contained only one good idea, I'd tear out the page with the good idea and throw the rest of the book away. And I'd put that idea to use.

Many books are written by people who are business writers and consultants. When you buy one of their books, you're buying a few hours of their time for a modest price. If you paid for one-on-one meetings with these people, it would cost hundreds or even thousands of dollars. If you attended one of their speeches or seminars, you still might pay more than a hundred dollars and only get to hear them for an hour or so. That's why, in my opinion, their books are bargains. That's also why, in the Resources section at the back of this book, there is a recommend list for those interested.

Now that we've talked about other books, let's discuss this one. There are many things about small business this book won't tell you. It won't tell you how to do a cash flow projection, how to decorate the windows of your retail store, how to comply with OSHA regulations on handling of hazardous chemicals, how to buy meat for your restaurant, or how to keep your forklift running when the main hydraulic seal blows out and you're in the middle of loading a rush order for your biggest customer. There are other books to deal with these specific matters.

This book covers the six areas which, from my observation, cause the most problems for business owners and managers. Five of those areas are: sales, marketing, customer service, employees, and general business management. The sixth area, "Now what?", or, "What do I do next now that the business is successful?", is an area that becomes a primary concern as your business matures. In my 10+ years of helping small- and mid-sized businesses, these areas are the ones that give owners the most headaches and the most sleepless nights.

Business owners and managers are too busy to read books during their business day. So they read them in the evening when they're tired after a full day's work. That's what I used to do. I can't tell you how many times I've been lying down reading a business book and fallen asleep only to be rudely awakened when the book fell out of my hands and hit me in the face. Those books really made an impression on me! Knowing that you'll be a little less than fully alert when you read this book, the chapters are deliberately short, so you'll be able to understand and finish a chapter before you can nod off. (If you feel sleepy, either put the book down or slip on a face guard!)

In an attempt to make the book more readable, true stories and confessions from my past to illustrate principles have been dredged up. Read a chapter or two at a time. Or, if you wish, read only those sections pertaining to the things that are giving you the most trouble in your business today. This book is not linear. You don't have to read Chapter 20 before you start Chapter 21. Use the Table of Contents to find the sections and chapters of most interest to you right now.

You should read this book in a special way. Consume it. Mutilate it. Mark relevant passages with a hi-liter marker. Make notes to yourself in the margins. Circle things that are especially relevant. Make lists of things to do as you are inspired by the book's ideas. When you're done, read it again — as often as you need to. It will help you make good decisions as your business grows and prospers.

Running a business or business segment is like raising dairy cattle — it is a continuous **task**. You can't just feed and milk your cows once or only when you have a few minutes to spare. They require constant, regular care. So does your business. You can't just formulate a business strategy or write a business plan and then forget it. You must change and evolve as your business grows, as the demographics of your marketplace shift, and as your competition changes. As your business grows and prospers, old problems and challenges will be replaced with new ones. Use the ideas and principles in this book to help you make changes and deal with problems. Now. Next year. Five years from now.

Make this book your friend for life.

How Not to Fail

The first rule of business success is: Don't Fail. If you fail, you'll never be successful. Sounds obvious, doesn't it? How many of us study the reasons for business failure in order to avoid it? Automotive safety engineers study car accidents in order to prevent future ones. For the same reason, you should learn about business failures in order to prevent a future one — yours!

Every year about 100,000 businesses in the United States fail. Dun & Bradstreet develops statistics on business failures that are updated yearly. While the percentages vary a bit from year to year, the reasons for business failure go something like this:

Disaster: 1 Percent. Some business failures are caused by fire, flood, or acts of God. No firm should go out of business for these reasons unless it has totally inadequate insurance protection. In 1980, when my small business was struggling to survive, a local pharmacy had a big fire. The owner was well-liked in the community and people took up a collection to help him rebuild. It was good he had made a lot of friends in town. I never contributed a dime. Even though I could barely pay myself a salary, I bought fire insurance on my business and disability insurance on myself and my partner. The pharmacist decided to forgo this to save a few bucks and, in my opinion, deserved to suffer the consequences. Enough money was raised so the pharmacist was able to rebuild and reopen. He continues to operate the business to this day, thanks to generosity and luck. Let's hope he bought some insurance this time around.

Fraud: 2 Percent. This means someone is stealing money from the company, usually a dishonest business partner or bookkeeper. I've met several people whose companies have been defrauded in a big way. In every case, they failed to keep an eye on the financial aspects of their business. They didn't like to deal with checkbooks or columns of numbers, leaving it for someone else to do. They didn't just delegate; they abdicated. They never looked at the figures in order to develop a feel for how the business should be doing. They never put controls in place to prevent diversion of funds or property. They invited fraud by having their heads in the sand and now they are paying dearly for it.

Neglect: 4 Percent. I once had a very good customer who was running a multi-million dollar wholesale business in the South. He had founded his business in the mid '50s and had built it up from nothing. In the late '80s, he decided he had worked long enough and moved to a resort area over a thousand miles away. "I can run this thing by fax and phone," he said. He delegated everything to three long-time employees. The problem was that for 30+ years this guy had run his business like a paranoid tyrant. He never delegated anything. His people were never given the chance to test their wings. He never shared the secrets of his success or trained them to run his business. He suddenly left the nest and said to his people, "Learn to fly and run it yourself." They tried and crashed. In less than two years, the business was broke because of neglect. I've seen others do the same, abdicating to their employees who have been given no direction or training. Fraud and neglect come from the same source — an unwillingness to face reality.

Lack of Line Experience: 10 Percent. In these cases, the owners have insufficient experience in their lines of work. A carpet cleaner who doesn't know how to clean carpets. A printer who doesn't understand the printing business. A technical writer who has a lousy writing style. You've probably experienced this kind of thing personally, wondering how a restaurant with such poor food can stay in business. The truth is, if they don't learn to serve good food before their savings run out, they'll be out of business. I know a woman who owned an upholstery repair business that she knew little about. When she went out and made calls on used car dealers to bid jobs, she frequently misquoted and misinterpreted what was needed. When her employees went out to do the work, they often took twice as long as she had figured. Therefore, many of the jobs were money-losers. Many of her customers were unhappy because she gave them unreasonable expectations about finished appearance. Her employees couldn't deliver on her promises and would end up arguing with the customer. Those customers took their future repair business elsewhere. She wouldn't take the time to learn the aspects of her business that she needed to know to do estimates properly and she soon went broke.

Unbalanced Experience: 22 Percent. Undoubtedly you've heard of businesses where the owner was a great salesperson but knew little about cost control and kept losing money until the business went under. Or a business where the owner knew a lot about accounting but couldn't sell his or her way out of a paper bag. The business never brought in enough revenues to cover its monthly operating costs. The company finally went under. Failures like these are the result of unbalanced experience on the part of the owner or manager. To successfully operate any business, you've got to bring a variety of skills to the table. You've got to wear several hats — salesperson, financial analyst, purchasing agent, personnel manager and more. Having skills in a single area alone isn't good enough. You've got to be flexible and versatile.

Managerial Incompetence: 61 Percent. Management is defined as the skillful use of resources to accomplish a purpose. Most small businesses have very limited resources, like money. It is, therefore, critical these limited means be skillfully used since there aren't any extra to waste. Most managerial incompetence is a combination of lack of skills and a poorly defined purpose. In the fall of 1957, when Ford Motor Company introduced the infamous Edsel automobile, they had ill-defined objectives and a lack of commitment to the project. Both of these problems ultimately killed the car. You'll read more about this in Chapter 20, Lessons from Detroit. Even though the Edsel died, Ford Motor Company itself survived because it had lots of money left to spend on more successful ventures. Big businesses can risk high dollar amounts on a project because the money spent is a relatively small portion of their total resources. Small businesses can't do this. Their assets are too small. They have to make good decisions. Many small businesses fritter away their assets because they make lots of bad decisions or, in some cases, no decisions.

A client once said to me, "Life is unfair. I'm the best decorator in this town but I'm barely making a living at it. It shouldn't be that way." This is a good illustration of the symptoms of business failures listed above. My client's technical competence as a decorator only gets her 10 percent of the way toward success. There are several reasons she's not successful. First, she has unbalanced experience. While she's a good decorator, she does a bad job of quoting. On some potentially lucrative jobs she wildly overbids and fails to get awarded the contract because her price is too high. On others, she underestimates how much time the job will take and ends up losing money. She has demonstrated lapses in managerial competence as well. She operates on a very limited advertising and promotional budget yet spends her ad money irregularly and emotionally, responding to the sales pitches of advertising reps rather than analyzing what ads work and what don't. She has no idea how new clients find out about her because she never asks. She is guilty of neglect, too. She always procrastinates and files her taxes late, which increases her cost of doing business because she's always paying penalties and late charges.

You may have heard the old saw, "If your business makes it through the first year, you'll succeed." Baloney! Less than 15 percent of all full-time, licensed businesses fail in the first year. About a third of all new businesses close their doors in the first three years. Yet 25 percent of the businesses that fail each year are more than 10 years old. In order to be successful over the long term you must be ever-vigilant. You can't get sloppy after a few years and expect your business to automatically prosper in the future.

Speaking of baloney, you'll occasionally meet former business owners who will tell you, "My business was doing fine until the recession came along and wiped me out." Here are the real facts about business failures during bad economic times. Business failures typically average four to five failures per 1,000 businesses in any normal year. That's a failure rate of one-half of one percent. In the recession of 1981 to 1983, the failure rate increased to nine out of 1,000 businesses. That's nine-tenths of one percent. During the Great Depression of the early 1930s, the annual failure rate was even higher — 12.5 per thousand. That's only one and one quarter percent. This means that, even during this awful economic period, 98¾ percent of all businesses did not fail each year. They survived. Only the ones that were already weak due to managerial incompetence or other shortcomings went under.

Pay attention to the principles, guidelines and suggestions that are discussed in this book — they'll help you prosper. They are the ingredients for making a great cake!

Back to Basics (What Makes a Business Successful)

In Chapter 2 you became an expert in business failure. (An expert is someone who has read something about a subject and can spout statistics about it. So, now you *are* one!) Since you already know what makes businesses fail, you should now learn what are the characteristics of successful businesses. Here are seven key characteristics of successful businesses:

1. A Bias for Action.

Successful owners and managers are decisive. They don't agonize or lose a lot of sleep rolling minor decisions around in their mind. They analyze the plusses and minuses of a situation, make a decision, and then implement it.

This is not to say that they're impulsive. Impulsive people make decisions because it "feels right" at the moment. If you asked them to justify their decision, they couldn't. Decisive people make decisions quickly but rationally. When asked, they can present logical reasons for their decision.

Rick is an accountant who wants more clients. I made five recommendations to him about changes to his marketing and promotional program that would greatly increase his client base. These changes would take eight hours of his time and cost about $200. Cheap and easy! It's been a year since Rick received these recommendations. He's never implemented any of them. When asked why, Rick said, "Well, I've thought about it a lot but I'm worried they might not all work." So what!?! If they don't work, Rick has lost a little time and a little money. Rick now needs even more clients because he's lost a half dozen that he hasn't been able to replace yet he's still twiddling his thumbs and doing nothing. Rick will never have a successful practice because he's too indecisive.

2. Outwardly Directed.

Those folks who are running good businesses don't spend all their time working inside their business. They go outside and make sure the inside of their business fits the outside world in which they operate. They keep in touch with customers through personal visits and by phone. They emphasize two-way communication. They talk and listen to their customers, suppliers and employees. They pay attention to what's going on in their industry by maintaining trade contacts, going to trade shows, and reading industry publications. They watch and analyze their competition.

I know of a janitorial company that has struggled to survive during the six years it's been in business. Hans, the owner, is always telling me how difficult it is to survive in this industry. "It's fiercely competitive," he says. "My competitors are a bunch of cutthroats. In my industry, you can't hire good people anymore. The customers are too demanding and won't pay enough." His available market has grown greatly over the last six years because a lot of new potential customers have relocated to his town. Yet Hans' business hasn't grown. When asked how his competitors manage to find good employees, he doesn't know. When asked if he ever went back and followed up with clients whose jobs he bid and lost to see if price was the real reason, he never has. "It's gotta be price. What else could it possibly be?" I once gave him a lead — a print shop that was looking for a new janitorial service. He never called them. I asked him why. He said, "I've been too busy trying to get my schedules straight. I'll get around to it sometime." That was over a year ago. Hans is a man who is inwardly directed. He has no idea what's going on outside of the minutiae of his business. He is doomed. Hans is destined to struggle forever in his small company or, at least, until he becomes so frustrated he throws in the towel and closes his doors.

3. Hands-On.

People who prosper in businesses have a "hands-on" approach to their company. That doesn't mean they spend their days performing every operation in the business. It means they are familiar with the various operations in the business. They may not actually *do* the books but they have an understanding of bookkeeping. They may not calculate the cash flow projections themselves but they know what cash flow means and have a feel for whether the specific numbers generated make sense. They may not do the physical inventory, but they have developed some rules-of-thumb for what the inventory should be. People with a hands-on approach delegate tasks but understand the tasks they delegate.

Jim, who owns a wholesale electronics business, is a good example of the hands-on approach. While visiting with him, he mentioned, "I just ran our monthly statements and there's something amiss. It shows that our inventory is up by 23 percent and I know that that's wrong." I asked how he knew. "I went out and looked in the warehouse and our shelves just don't look that full. Besides, I did a quick check of our sales and purchases and our inventory should be, if anything, down a little." Jim later found two clerical errors caused the inventory reporting mistake. Jim has a good enough "feel" for his business to be able to spot discrepancies quickly and correct them.

4. Hires Good People and Keeps Them.

"A company is only as good as its people." Everyone has heard this. You may be annoyed that I'm feeding you an ancient cliché, but it's a true one. You can't have a good business if you have a lot of mediocre employees. They'll drive away customers, make too many errors, and drive you nuts because they're undependable and untrustworthy. Chapter 32 shows you how to hire and keep good people.

Pete, one of my clients, runs a $3 million per year machinery manufacturing business. He delegates a lot of his work so he can devote some time to his antique collecting hobby. He's away from the business a lot but has good people working for him. When I need to reach him, I just call Susan. She knows the business inside and out and she can answer almost all of my questions. If she can't, Susan knows how to reach Pete and relay his answer to me.

5. High Overall Business Productivity.

Whether you measure their efforts in sales dollars per sales employee, net profits per square foot of retail space, or return on assets, successful companies have scores significantly higher than their business peers.

These companies have learned to deploy their assets (financial assets, people assets, physical plant assets) to produce outstanding returns.

Fred and Don run a sales rep agency. They realize the only way to be productive is to deploy their reps efficiently. They support their eight field people with three inside sales people who provide back-up. These people handle inquiries, send out literature, qualify prospects, and schedule appointments. Every field salesperson has a cellular phone to retrieve voice mail and call customers from the field. They have an ever expanding sales database that is available to all reps through their sales contact software. The company constantly tinkers with its compensation system, offering special bonuses and awards for exceptional productivity. Fred and Don are in the upper quartile of sales agencies nationwide for dollar sales per sales rep and overall agency profitability. It pays to be productive.

6. Deliver What They Promise — Nothing Less.

Successful businesses have systems in place to make sure they keep their commitments. They put tickler systems in place to deal with back orders. If they think something will be ready on Tuesday, they tell the customer Wednesday — that way if the system fails they've bought themselves a day of grace. They will lose money on an order rather than break a promise. They provide their employees with pleasant surprises — not unpleasant ones. They never try to weasel out of commitments to suppliers, customers, or employees.

In 1983, my company quoted a $15,000 store display job to a major retailer. The delivery date was critical. Material had to be special ordered. We placed the order with the factory that told us the material was in stock and would ship within two days. When it didn't arrive, we called again and were told, "Whoops, it was promised to someone else. So we shipped it to them. Guess we should have told you, but we have some in our warehouse in Houston, Texas." In order for us to meet our delivery commitment, we had to have the material air freighted to us at a cost of $2,600. The supplier refused to cover the freight. We paid it. We kept our commitment to our customer. We also showed them the freight bill and said, "With $2,600 in unexpected costs on a $15,000 job, we obviously didn't make any money on this one, but when we give our word, we keep it. We hope that you'll let us quote your next order." They did. It was that kind of attitude that helped us grow and helped our company develop a loyal customer following. Oh, about that supplier. By refusing to own up to their problem, they lost our trust. They paid that $2,600 many times over in lost future sales.

7. Keep Trying Until Something Works.

Successful entrepreneurs never bet the farm on any one thing. They try things and tinker and measure results. They dabble in markets to see if they're viable before they commit a lot of resources to them. They keep testing new things and measuring results. This characteristic is so important and so often overlooked, that it deserves its own chapter. So please turn the page and read on.

Keep Trying Until Something Works

While giving a talk to a group of start-up business owners, the question arose, "In your experience of owning businesses and counseling small business owners, what is the one most important thing they need to do?" Without thinking, I blurted out, "Keep trying until something works." My answer was spontaneous but it revealed some deep-seated feelings about start-up businesses and small businesses in general. Small businesses don't just grow; they evolve. Frequently they evolve in directions the owner never expected.

There are two reasons behind this phenomenon. The first is Murphy's Law. Things don't work out as you plan them. People who you thought would turn from prospects into clients, patrons, or customers don't. They talk a good game but they never buy. Perhaps your bank loan doesn't get approved. (Banks are famous for mouthing soothing, non-committal phrases which *you* mistakenly interpret to mean agreement.) Maybe the location you picked out is no longer available, or the prospective partner you were talking with gets cold feet. Expect the unexpected. As Murphy said, "If anything can go wrong, it will."

The second reason businesses evolve in unexpected directions is because a new opportunity presents itself. You get a chance to buy a bankrupt business for pennies on the dollar. A prospect turns you on to a new market for your product or service. A market you've been ignoring turns out to be just right for you. Here's an example:

When my partner and I first started our plastics business, we thought we had found a hole in the market to fill. We were both mechanical engineers by training and plastics experts by experience. We felt there was a real need for a company that could competently design and build research vessels, laboratory devices, and test equipment from clear plastic. We had seen a lot of poorly-designed equipment that failed because the shops producing the equipment had no real understanding about the behavior of plastic materials under stress. We pictured ourselves sitting around a conference table in fine leather chairs, smoking cigars, and sipping brandy discussing technical matters with fellow engineers, guiding them in the proper design and application of plastics. HA! The reality was that most of our discussions were in the alley behind our business, making sketches on the back of an envelope, and sipping lukewarm coffee from a paper cup while our prospect smoked a cigarette. We did get some technical and design business but when Ronald Reagan won the White House in 1980, he cut many of the Jimmy Carter-style federal grants and programs, which funded the type of research that used our products. We were now starving and had to do something different.

We began producing vacuum-formed plastic components for medical and electronic manufacturers. That worked but we had to keep finding new customers. Small, start-up companies would use vacuum-formed pieces for their initial production. If their product was successful they would then switch to injection-molded components, which had significantly higher tooling costs but had far lower unit costs. If their product was unsuccessful, they'd just go out of business. Either way, we'd lose the customer.

Then we looked at making plastic skylights for residences. We did a market survey; it looked promising. So we spent some money on a prototype tool. Then we went out surveying again, this time with samples of our proposed product. We were ready to take advance orders so we could tool up for full production. In the nine weeks following our initial survey, two new players had jumped into the market and driven down prices by 15 percent. This wrecked havoc with our profit projections. Based on this new development, we chose not to enter the market. Good thing we didn't, too. Both competitors went out of business within two years and dragged three other companies down with them. We also tried our hand at selling plastic signs, nameplates, and badges through stationery and office products dealers (more on this in Chapter 11), but it was a market with limited profit potential. Then, we fell backwards into the display market.

A friend of ours at Quality Plastics, a plastic injection-molder, was asked to bid a plastic point-of-purchase display job for the phone company. He passed the bid request on to us. We quoted the job. Two weeks later we got a call from Pacific Northwest Bell saying, "Congratulations. We don't know who you are but you were the low bidder of 21 other bids and you've got the job. Oh, by the way, we're increasing the quantities we need by 50 percent. We need delivery in four weeks." Holy cow! The first thing I did was race back to my office and recheck the quote. I was sure we had made a big math error and were going to lose our shirts on the job. Well, there was no math error and we made a nice profit on our work. We thought we might be on to something here and started chasing more display work.

Our display business grew and grew. It became a nice, profitable business segment for us. Over a period of a few years we junked the skylight tools, got rid of the vacuum-forming machine, sold the sign and badge-making portion of our business and quit making laboratory tanks and vessels. When we sold our company nine years later, about 90 percent of our business was display-related.

While we tried many things, we never bet the farm on any one thing. We held back capital and energy in order to have a reserve so we could try something else in case things didn't work out. You can't keep trying until something works if you run out of money. We were careful. We never jumped into a market until we tested the water with our toes first. We tried to find low-cost ways to test new products and new markets (see Chapter 7).

Do you think this story is unique? Well, it's not. It happened again, when I started my next business. I decided to start a video production company specializing in making business videos as a training and sales tool. During a sales call, the prospect would explain his or her ideas and needs. As often as not, I'd suggest using a brochure, a series of printed case studies, a slide presentation, or a direct mail piece. This is not a great way to sell video services — telling customers that they shouldn't buy them! If your business is video production, you certainly shouldn't use this technique! In reality, I had evolved into a marketing consultant. People were paying me for my marketing advice. When I'd be out pitching my marketing expertise, I'd end up working on employee problems, productivity issues, financing requirements, or customer service needs.

I had evolved again into a general business advisor. That's what I do today, and I'm enjoying every minute of it!

I've seen accounting firms turn into computer consultants; automobile restorers who closed down their restoration facility and concentrated on remanufacturing electrical parts for old cars; hobby shops that evolved into manufacturers and importers of fine, fully-built models of cars, trains and planes with a nationwide distribution network; restaurants that bolted the front door and focused on an outside catering service; a supplier of automotive original equipment parts who told Ford and GM to take a hike and began producing items for gift shops — at much higher margins.

Baseball legend Babe Ruth struck out 1,330 times, but he kept trying. Abraham Lincoln was defeated six times in his quest for political office before becoming president of the U.S. Thomas Edison tried thousands of filaments before finding one that was satisfactory for use in a light bulb. He kept trying until he found one that worked while learning something from every unsuccessful attempt.

Banking giant Citicorp began as a private credit union. Phillip Morris started as a retail tobacconist in London. They manufactured their first cigarette seven years later. Boeing made furniture and speedboats while developing a commercially acceptable plane. Marriott Corporation began as an A&W Root Beer stand. Wal-Mart started as a Ben Franklin five-and-dime franchisee. Nordstrom was, at first, just another little shoe store in Seattle.

None of these business transformations took place overnight. All of these companies evolved into something else gradually. They were presented with opportunities and took advantage of them. Or they were given a lemon and chose to make lemonade. Those who own and operate so-so, ho-hum businesses always scoff at these nimble and successful entrepreneurs and say, "Aaaahh, they were just lucky."

Richard LaMotta, who founded Chipwich, Inc. (maker of ice cream sandwiches made with chocolate chip cookies) in the early '80s, said it best. "There's no such thing as luck or timing. You create it yourself. Preparation meets opportunity — that's what you call luck. Keep your eye out for new opportunities for your business. Be prepared. Luck will follow."

Business Management

Management is the skillful use of resources to accomplish a purpose. In any small business, resources are limited. Therefore it is important to be exceedingly skillful in using these resources.

If you're a big company, like IBM or General Motors, you can sometimes deploy your resources in a very stupid manner and still survive. We know this to be true because both companies did exactly that in the '70s and '80s yet they started fixing their problems and are now thriving again. Most small companies who deployed their resources stupidly in the 1980s are no longer in business.

As a small business you have a limited amount of cake mix to work with, so you'd better manage it well and learn quickly from any of your cake-making attempts. In the following chapters, we'll concentrate on helping you to use your resources wisely.

You Can't Save the Company on Weekends Anymore

In the early days of our manufacturing company, my business partner and I used to save our little company every weekend. We'd forget to get a job done during the week, and come in on Saturday and Sunday to complete it. We might have to re-do a job that we had messed up, or to quote some job that we didn't have time to deal with during the week. If we didn't do these things, we were sure our customers would get mad and leave us, and the company would die. We'd have to save the company the next weekend, too, because we'd be so exhausted from working hard the week before we'd make more mistakes the following week and have to rectify them the following weekend.

I don't know what the defining event was that made us stop this cycle of failure. Maybe we just got so sick and tired of not having any personal lives outside the company we simply said, "If the company can't make it during the week, it deserves to die." In any case, we stopped working so hard in the business. That gave us more time to work on the business. We now had the time to set up cost control systems, to evaluate employees, to fire the ones who made most of the mistakes (except, of course, ourselves), and to praise and reward the good ones. We had time to make a business plan, to set goals, and take actions. We not only wrote a business plan, we stuck to it, too. We now had the time and the inclination to pull our business plan out of the file and act on it.

This gave us a chance to re-evaluate our customers, too. We learned to work hard to keep the good ones and get rid of the bad ones. We had the time to ask our good customers questions about how we could do a better job for them. We learned from our customers' comments and made appropriate changes to better serve them. We stopped over-promising on jobs we took; if customers had unreasonable deadlines, we told them we couldn't meet them. We gave our customers realistic completion dates for work we accepted, and we set up schedule boards to keep jobs on track in order to meet our commitments. We felt better about our business and less frustrated. We had a life outside the business, too, and our families got to know us again.

We hired more people to take care of the things we still didn't have time to do ourselves, figuring this would increase our overhead and, therefore, lower our profits. We were willing to pay that price to keep the business from driving us nuts. Surprisingly, it didn't work out that way. The profits actually increased, because our employees were doing a better job than we ever did. They weren't tired and brought fresh ideas and new viewpoints to our business. We hired even more employees and made even more money. This gave us even more time to work on our business and allowed us to try some new marketing strategies. They worked. The strategies made us more money that we reinvested in talented people, who made us more money, and so on.

When we sold the business, it was 36 times bigger than when we bought it. The company that purchased our business may have thought they were just buying our corporate stock, our inventory, and our customer list. They weren't. They were buying access to the pool of talent that we had hired and the systems we had established to motivate those talented people. Most of the people and the systems are still in place today and the company continues to grow. The new owners doubled the size of the company in less than five years. They tell me this year's sales are up over 26 percent and our former little company is their most profitable division.

What about your company? Are you still trying to save it every weekend? If so, you're doomed to running in place. You won't grow but your problems will until they overwhelm you, or they make you so frustrated and tired you throw in the towel. Don't let this happen! Start working *on* your business so you can make it a success. Take this weekend off and think about what you want your business to become. Then, next week, start steering it in that direction. Begin by hiring good people to help you make your business grow and succeed. You'll never regret it.

Remembering the Somat Machine

L ast night I dreamed about the Somat machine, something I hadn't thought about it in quite a while. In the early '70s, I worked in a big downtown office building for the plastic department of a Fortune 500 company and I frequently received plastic samples from our laboratory. When I finished evaluating the samples, I usually threw them away. One morning I got a call from someone who said, "We want you to stop throwing that plastic stuff in your wastebasket. The Somat machine can't digest it and it gets clogged up. So cut it out."

My first question was, of course, "What the heck is a Somat machine?" It was a special machine that took paper trash and mixed it with water and chemicals and turned it into a slushy pulp. My company had installed this machine in the basement of the building and they had a big tanker truck show up every day to haul away the pulp, which they sold to a paper company. The company bought the Somat because they thought it would save them money — instead of paying to have trash hauled away, they would pulp it and sell it. This was quite a progressive concept in the early '70s; recycling was not a very big deal in those days.

My second question was, "How did someone track me down as the person throwing plastic in the trash?" In a nine-story office building with thousands of wastebaskets, this was a formidable task. The answer was the Somat Police.

How did a company get from a simple cost-saving device to a bureaucracy with its own police force? The answer is one little step at a time. When the company purchased the machine they needed someone to operate it, so they hired an individual I'll call Somatman. Somatman fell in love with the machine and wanted to become more knowledgeable, so he asked the company to pay for his membership in The Somat Society (TSS). The company agreed. Then Somatman wanted to attend TSS technical conferences. The company agreed to that, too. These conferences were always held in far-away places, like Geneva, Hong Kong and Cairo. So Somatman spent a lot of time flying between continents in the first-class section of airplanes, thinking up ways to build his Somat Empire. At that time, it was company policy that employees could travel first-class on overseas flights. Since somebody had to run the machine while Somatman was away, he hired an assistant whom I'll call Little Somat.

Somatman wrote technical papers on the performance of the Somat machine. One was to be delivered in Rio de Janeiro and Somatman wanted visuals for his presentation, so he had slides shot by the company photographer. The Marketing Division had to hire outside photographers for two new pieces of sales literature because the company photographer was too busy shooting interesting angles of the Somat machine. After the technical papers were delivered, Somatman had reprints made by the company's in-house print shop to give to his friends, colleagues, and fellow TSS members. Meanwhile the Finance Division had to have the third quarter stockholders report printed outside because the company print shop was too busy to run it.

Somatman decided the Somat machine was a great public relations device, so he had Little Somat give free tours to citizen groups, social organizations, and schoolchildren. They cordoned off the area with velvet ropes and brass poles, had the Somat room painted and decorated and ordered souvenirs in the shape of a little Somat machine that were molded out of indigestible plastic and imprinted with the company logo. Of course, they couldn't actually *run* the machine while tours were being given — it was too noisy and the chemicals smelled. So they now had a hard time keeping up with the waste paper generated by the company. Somatman and Little Somat never ran the machine themselves because they were too busy traveling and giving tours. They hired others to actually do the work. They also hired a consultant who studied the process and recommended they purchase a second Somat machine to increase their capacity.

Somatman was delighted and took the consultant's report and had fancy graphs and charts made by the graphics department to make a presentation to management. Management approved the second Somat machine purchase, although at the same meeting they turned down a request for a pelletizing extruder needed to increase manufacturing capacity for their fastest-selling product. It was probably because the presentation graphs weren't very good. The head of the Manufacturing Division tried to get the graphics department to make some charts but they said they were all booked up. He had to do them himself and they looked pretty lame next to Somatman's nice charts.

The Somat consultant also recommended that security procedures should be tightened around the two Somat machines since they were dealing with valuable documents containing company-confidential information. A security force was established. In order to differentiate them from regular corporate security they were given different uniforms with special ecru (pulp-colored) berets and shoulder braids. Since no terrorist groups seemed to be interested in the Somat machines, the Somat Police spent most of their time looking spiffy for tour groups, checking wastebaskets, tracking down offenders who placed improper trash in their receptacles, and intimidating them.

Do you think this sort of thing could only happen at a big company? Well, think again! When I was running my wholesale business in the '80s, I offered free delivery to small customers. I'd call prospects on Tuesday and get orders, load up my van with goods on Tuesday evening, and start delivering early Wednesday morning. I'd finish by noon, pick up merchandise that was needed for my shop in the afternoon, and drive back to the shop. It was very efficient. Part of the deal with the free delivery was I'd personally pick up checks from my customers on the spot. No invoicing, no collection problems. Many of these people were very small businesses with shaky credit.

Then I got busy and delegated the phoning to one person and the delivery to someone else and forgot about it until later that year when my delivery guy had an accident and the van was damaged to the tune of $600. How much product did he deliver that day? Only $400! Holy cow! I used to deliver $2,500 in one morning. Well, at least I got the checks. What's this — only $200? "Well, two of them said they didn't have their checkbook handy." Yes, and they were my worst-paying customers, too. I realized I had my own version of the Somat Empire in my small company. The reason that I had started my free delivery service in the first place was to efficiently and economically serve a batch of small accounts. That was no longer the case. Over time, the delivery service had evolved into something else — an inefficient money-loser. We began shipping only by common carrier and paid the freight if the order exceeded $500. Guess what? A lot of my small customers got together and pooled their orders to get the freight paid. My slow-pay customers got their shipments COD and I kept their business, too. Everything worked out OK. My company got out of the delivery business because we weren't good at it anymore — and it was no longer meeting our needs.

How about you? Do you have the equivalent of a Somat machine in your business? Something that started out with the best of intentions but turned into a monster? If so, make some changes. Simplify your business life. Stick to doing what you do best.

As for me, I still think about the Somat machine now and then. Whenever I travel to a large city and see some big tanker truck tying up downtown traffic during rush hour, I always wonder if it's hauling pulp from someone's Somat Empire!

·   ·   ·

AUTHOR'S NOTE: This story is a compilation of numerous events in my life at one big company. There was no single individual known as Somatman, but there were many Somatmen in this big company traveling to meaningless conferences at resorts. They'd hire Little Somats to do their grunt-work while they were off having a good time. Their staff may not have had uniforms, but they had squads of syncophants whose sole job was to intimidate people in other departments with meaningless tripe. I saw many instances where important work was underfunded so money could be siphoned off for someone's unprofitable and silly pet project. I witnessed many programs that began with good intentions deteriorate and become unstoppable monsters that had outlived their usefulness. And I really did get calls from the Somat Department complaining about plastic samples in my wastebasket. Yes, Virginia, there is a Somat machine!

The Legacy of
William B. Stout

William Bushnell Stout was a prodigious engineer and inventor. Aviation historians know him as the builder of the 1919 Batwing, which was the first commercial American monoplane and as the father of the Ford Trimotor airplane. The Trimotor was the first production passenger airplane designed with a metal skin instead of cloth, wire and wood. In a way, Bill Stout helped to create commercial air travel by developing a reliable commercial aircraft made with durable materials.

Automobile buffs may remember the Stout Scarab of the early 1930s. This unique vehicle is the grandfather of today's modern minivan. Bill Stout's Scarab had many futuristic features not seen in other '30s cars such as four wheel independent suspension, hidden door hinges, push button door locks, flush glass, fully enclosed wheels, no running boards, and flush aero headlights.

As an inventor and small business owner, Bill Stout offered some words that are applicable to today's small business environment. Bill said, "Never resort to mathematics until you have exhausted all the possibilities of a couple of toothpicks and a piece of string." What Bill meant is you don't need to analyze a new idea to death; frequently, you can try some low budget experiments to test your idea.

If you're in the restaurant business and you want to add some ethnic food items to your menu but you're not sure if your customers are interested, you can print up a small run of special item menus and clip them to your regular menus. Then you can measure what people order and determine the popularity of these dishes. You can keep experimenting until you find a combination that works. Cactus Ya Ya, a restaurant in Vancouver, Washington, specializes in Mexican and Southwestern cuisine. They also offer eclectic fare such as garlic mashed potatoes and Philadelphia cheese steaks. It works for them.

In the wholesale segment of my plastics business, we decided to try a price-cutting tactic to see if we would gain more business. We registered a fictitious name, placed a small ad in the yellow pages and put in an extra phone line with its own number. Then we placed a small ad in the yellow pages. Our slogan was "Before you buy, call us for a quote!" We were disappointed in the results of the campaign and axed it a few months later. Nevertheless, it was an economical experiment, costing less than $700, that didn't sully the name of our regular business. We moved on to more promising programs, but at least we had tried another tactic.

Mail order experts say you can't accurately test the statistical pull of a mailing list or an offer unless you mail at least 5,000 pieces. That's true, but if you send, say, 500 pieces and you get some response then, by all means, scale up and do a full-blown test. If you get absolutely no response, the market is telling you something. Shut down your direct mail program and re-think it. Is there a problem with the offer in your mailing? Or maybe you've got a bad mailing list. Think about it before you spend more money.

If you've got a new product idea, you don't need to fly all over the nation to try it out. Chances are there's someone within easy driving distance of your office who's a potential customer for your idea. Buy them lunch and solicit their opinion. They'll probably be flattered you asked and provide you with valuable feedback.

Before we ever embarked on filling a production order for displays in our plastics business, we made a hand-made plastic prototype to get the OK from our customer. Before we did that, we made a "quick and dirty" sample out of cardboard and masking tape, using a box knife. It only took us a few minutes but it told us whether the proportions were right, the size made sense and whether the part was stable enough so it wouldn't tip over. These were all things you couldn't tell from a two dimensional sketch. While we were using cardboard and masking tape instead of toothpicks and string, we were following the philosophy of the legendary Mr. Stout.

Bill Stout's lesson is very applicable to running your own business. Don't be afraid to experiment, especially if it doesn't cost much to do so. Don't wait and vacillate. Try something new now!

Are You Being
Efficient or Just Tapping
a Dead Pope on the Head?

In the Holy Roman Catholic Church there is a special ceremony that takes place when a Pope dies. The Vatican Secretary of State takes a small silver hammer and taps on the forehead of the dead pontiff, calling his name, and asking in Latin, "Are you dead?" The hammer strike and the question is repeated three times; only then, in the eyes of the Roman Catholic Church, is the Pope considered dead. This ritual dates back many centuries. This may seem obsolete in this age of EKGs and EEGs and other marvels of medical measurement; there are far more reliable ways of determining death these days. But the ritual continues simply because it *is* a ritual — a symbol of and connection with the Catholic Church of ages ago.

Ceremonies and rituals are important to all religions. They are the pattern of the fabric of religious tradition and, perhaps, proof that the ceremonies and values of various religions transcend the fads and fetishes of today's secular world. When you look at your business as part of that secular world, age-old ceremonies and traditions may be the last thing you want. Especially if you're trying to run your business more efficiently.

As a business consultant, I'm exposed to many ceremonies in big and small companies. Most of these rituals have lost all meaning and relevance to the business. They exist because "we've always done it this way." Here are some examples:

Many companies tabulate numbers every month that no one understands. A wholesaler measures "will-call" sales as a percentage of overall sales. Why? No one knows. Has this ratio ever been used to try and shift sales one way or the other? Nope. "We've been making this calculation for years; we have a lot of history there." So what? Who cares!

"These people buy from us less than once every five years, so we only schedule them for yearly in-person calls." Why? If they buy that infrequently, why go see them at all? Why not telephone them once per year — it's cheaper. Why not judge them not just on their order frequency but their dollar value? If they only buy every six years but they order $800,000 worth of goods, shouldn't they be treated differently than someone who buys $75 worth of merchandise every eight years?

"We open at 10:00 A.M. and close at 5:30 P.M. because everyone else on the street does." Oh yeah? My son once owned a comic book store in a retail strip in a small college town in Oregon and his store's hours were from noon to 6:00 P.M. because that's when his customers came in to buy.

"We have our staff meeting Friday — we always have." Why? Is anything of value accomplished at that meeting, or does it just drone on and on? Maybe everyone should stand up for the entire meeting; at least, it will keep the meeting short. Maybe it should be held every two weeks, or monthly, or not at all.

A client of mine who was running a multi-million dollar printing business insisted on checking every invoice, every job ticket, and every quotation for errors. Why? Because her dad always did this when he was running the business. When her dad was running the business, gross revenues were only $100,000 per year or so and everything was done manually. Today, the business is much larger. Quotations, job cost data, and invoicing is all done with software. She spends 15 to 20 hours each week checking for errors. In the past six months she's caught $575 worth of billing errors and 15 spelling mistakes. Her recovery rate is $1.26 per hour. She needs to abandon this family ceremony and spend her time running the company.

Remember, you're not running a religion; you're running a business. Question every ceremony and ritual you have. If they've outlived their usefulness, get rid of them. Throw out that silver hammer, too, if you have one.

"I Got Just One Word for Ya Kid — Plastics!"

We all laughed at that line in the movie, *The Graduate*. Here was some know-it-all 40-something passing on his mundane version of the wisdom-of-the-period to a perplexed Dustin Hoffman. When the movie first came out in 1967, my laboratory co-workers and I laughed especially hard since we were working on the cutting edge of the plastics industry. Plastics were still miracle materials back in those days.

Having a plastics business in the '60s was almost like having a license to print money. People who worked in the plastics industry were looked at with awe, like people in information technology are today. Of course times changed, the plastics industry matured and people in the plastics business now have to fight to make a living the same way metal benders, woodworkers, and most of the rest of us do. You may find the words of wisdom from plastics industry leaders profiled in a recent issue of *Plastics World* magazine interesting as these comments and recommendations are very applicable to every business, not just the plastics trade.

John R. Weeks, president of Precise Technology, a producer of medical packaging with $35 million in sales, says, "You must have a plan. Don't try to be all things to all customers in all markets. Make choices, chart a course, don't drift but, rather, steer your business toward the millennium." Sounds like good advice for almost any business or practice from homebuilding to optometry. You are in charge of your business. It's up to you to determine the future direction of your business. If you don't, it will drift aimlessly propelled by the winds of selfishness from your worst employees or the tidal pulls of your least loyal customers.

Richard Crawford, president and CEO of Cambridge Industries, a privately-held molder of plastic automotive parts with 11 U.S. plants, believes companies that survive "will be strong in design, engineering, program management, continuous improvement, and innovation." Being innovative is important whether you have 11 big factories or one small one. Don't stagnate in your thinking. Improve your business. Make it better and you'll keep your old customers and attract new ones. Innovation and improvement will make your business an exciting place to work. You'll attract good people — and keep them as employees. You'll make your business stronger and you'll have more fun running it.

Steven Murrill of Profile Plastics of Northbrook, Illinois says, "What else can you do? Expand your capabilities. Examine your core strengths. Seek out customers and markets that need your core strengths and investigate what it will take to satisfy their needs." Good idea. Have you examined your strengths lately? Ask yourself why customers seek your products or services instead of those of your competitors. How can you capitalize on your unique strengths and advantages? You need to do this whether you've got a manufacturing plant, a retail store, or run a service business from your home.

In *The Graduate*, Dustin Hoffman's character never did become a plastics magnate. He did set a goal and, by the end of the movie, took the actions needed to reach his objective — Mrs. Robinson's daughter! He didn't let Mrs. Robinson stand in his way. In the pursuit of your business goals, don't you let anyone or anything stand in your way, either!

Joysticks
and Blinking Lights

The day the big Hendricksaw arrived was memorable. It was a fully automatic panel saw and the most expensive piece of machinery our company had ever bought. The Hendricksaw cost almost $50,000 and we were all anxious to see it working. We weren't disappointed. It had air clamps that went wooosh, a feeder/positioner that went whirrrrr, lots of colored lights that blinked on and off, a big digital readout that went to four decimal places, and a joystick controller to play with. It was painted a silvery grey color and had big, bright decals on the sides. It was massive; it took up a 10 by 20 foot space and stood out from everything else in the shop. It was very impressive to customers and I always made sure that I showed it off to my friends, too. "Look at this, Bert ... cost 50 grand, ya know. Isn't it cool!" The new saw also made our plant more efficient; it paid for itself in about 18 months or so.

In our company, we had other equipment, too. One was a special edge-finishing machine, which didn't look very impressive. It was about the size of a medium-size copy machine, painted a nondescript beige color, and had an on/off switch and two dials. It cost $24,000 but it paid for itself in three months. Eventually, we bought three of these little wonders but I had trouble getting excited about them.

When I placed my second order, we asked the factory, "Can we order this with some lights that blink on and off?" No. "How about a digital readout instead of those dials?" Sorry. "Well, could you put a big decal, some racing stripes or something on it?" Not available. We ordered it anyway but I never showed it to Bert.

In business, it's important to remember the reason for being in business is to make profits first rather than play with toys and impress your friends. I've heard people say things like, "I didn't get any orders shipped today but I got the UPS scale fine-tuned." Or, "I didn't make any sales calls today but I got the video editing equipment recalibrated so if customers ever come in and want some special video effects, we're ready for them." HEY! Stop playing with your toys! You're not going to get paid until you ship those orders and you're not going to do any video business unless you get out there and find some clients.

Dan operates a wholesale hardware business in Portland, Oregon. It's a very small company — just Dan and one employee. It is a low-margin business with just a few products. The business does about $400,000 in annual sales and barely breaks-even. Dan needs to double his sales volume with his present products and add a few higher margin items to his line. Dan has some ideas about new products to add but needs to do a little market survey with his customers. He could easily double his sales since his market share is very small. He just needs to get on the phone and call more prospects and ask for orders. Dan hasn't made a sales call in six months because he's been busy installing and learning to use a computer. He has now developed great little pie charts telling him exactly how badly his business is doing!

When I recommended to Dan that he turn off his computer for two weeks and go sell his wares, he was taken aback. "Information is the key to success," he said. That may be right, but in Dan's case, the best way to get information is to call up some customers and ask them how much they would like to buy today. That's what is important to his business.

Ted laughed when he saw my big Rolodex in the office. "Get with it, Joe, it's the '90s," he said, pulling out his pocket-sized electronic Rolodex. Ted had all the latest equipment and could pull up year-to-date financial statements in a flash. However, he had no idea what his individual job costs were in his wood products manufacturing plant. His method of quoting was "by guess and by golly" and he hadn't made a profit in 14 months.

I showed Ted a very simple manual job cost program. He looked at it with disdain. "You mean you don't have a computerized version of this?" I explained that the system was easily adapted to off-the-shelf job-cost software but it was important that he get something in place now.

His company was hemorrhaging money because some jobs were big losers and Ted didn't know which ones they were. Ted passed on my advice. Like Nero fiddling away while Rome burned, he played with his gadgets and overlooked the obvious until his creditors forced him into bankruptcy seven months later. The company closed its doors and his equipment and toys were auctioned off. One of my clients got a good deal on Ted's computer system; the first thing he did was install job-cost software.

A prospect of mine grabbed my business card and entered the data in her PDA (an electronic Personal Digital Assistant). It took her over four minutes to enter my name, address, phone, and fax. I've had shoes resoled faster than that! When she asked for my opinion of her electronic toy, I commented that my former business partner, John, used to take business cards and staple them to a Rolodex card and file them on his Rolodex wheel. She was miffed — feeling that I had insulted her electronic gizmo.

Perhaps there's someone out there reading this who's thinking, "What is this guy talking about? I'm in a service business; I don't have toys to play with." Oh, yeah? Well, what about that meeting last week when you were going to show me some data?

"I think it's in the data folder in my laptop computer," you said. "I'll bring it up now. Let's see ... I'll just scroll through this stuff here ... Well, I guess it's not in this folder. Oh, wait. I bet I can get it from the accounts file; I'll just hit the F10 key. Whooops ... I think there's a freeze up here ... let me re-boot and we'll try accessing through F2. Whoa! I didn't know it could do this, too; look at these cool pie charts. Uh Oh! What's this? Low Battery Warning! Are you kidding? I just charged that sucker the other day."

Meanwhile, the data you wanted to show me was also on a piece of paper in your desk. You could have retrieved it in 10 seconds. Now who's playing with toys? And what about all the calls you're making on your cellular phone? Are they really important business calls or are you just ordering a pizza-to-go from your car?

Computers can be a great help in communicating with others in business. E-mail is invaluable when properly used. The Internet can be an excellent source of business information. But too many people are on the

Net finding pen pals instead of developing business contacts. And despite the growth of the Internet and the derisive comments about "snail mail," as a nation we're buying more Post-Its® than ever.

The point is: When you buy equipment, make sure you're buying a tool not a toy. Use your equipment as a tool to make your business better, not just as a gadget to amuse you, and amaze your friends.

The Worst Thing
in Your Business

*(Just as many hotels never have a 13th floor because it's bad luck, maybe busi-
ness books shouldn't have anything called Chapter 11. Here's hoping that
reading this Chapter 11 will help prevent your business from ever filing a
Chapter 11 bankruptcy petition.)*

Lots of people write about long-term business planning and with good
reason. Long-term planning is very important for your business
though it doesn't mean much when you're up to your neck in water and
still trying to bail out the boat. Of course, that's how every small business owner spends a lot of his or her day. You don't need grandiose
plans, you just need *one* thing you can do right away to make a real and
immediate improvement in your business. Here's an idea.

The best way to make an immediate improvement in your business is to
get rid of the worst thing in your business right now. No one knows
what the worst thing in your business is, except you. It the thing that dri-
ves you nuts during the day. It gives you headaches and makes you
leave the business to go buy some aspirin. It keeps you awake at night.
Whatever it is, get rid of it now.

My business came with a little lapel badge and nameplate engraving
business attached as a sideline. It was a nice little business segment and
profitable, although it never really grew very much. As other segments
of my business grew, it became a real nuisance. The badge business was-
n't big enough to assign a production employee to it full time. One of my
employees would be pulled off other work to make badges and nameplates when orders came in. One day, when we were trying to get out a

very big production order making point-of-purchase displays for Hewlett-Packard, someone from the Ladies Bowling League was screaming at me because her $4 name tag wasn't finished. H-P gives me a $35,000 order and five weeks to produce it; the Bowling League lady gives me a $4 order and gives me one day to produce it. What's wrong with this picture!?! Nameplates and badges had now become the worst thing in my business. We sold off the engraving business to a local trophy shop and focused on our primary business, plastic displays. It was a great sense of relief. The Bowling League Ladies now had a good supplier who was geared up to deliver their orders in one day and, most importantly, I had gotten rid of the worst thing in my business.

For some companies, the worst thing in the business is a particular customer. Customers exist who are unreasonable, petty, mean-spirited, slow payers and abusive. You probably have a few. You've never gotten rid of them because you've read all those inspirational, well-meaning business books that tell you to never, never walk away from a potential sale. You get mad at your staff when they're downtrodden and grumpy after dealing with this bozo customer and you worry that your staff may telegraph their suppressed rage to the next customer or prospect they encounter. Stop worrying by getting rid of your worst customer right now!

Sometimes, the worst thing in your business has a name. Like Fred, Julie, Murray, or Amy. Why is it we're so decisive about defects in products or merchandise but wishy-washy about defective employees? If you've got an employee who is not doing what you want, act now. Set performance goals and a short timetable. If they don't come up to par, replace them. If they're truly a bad employee, get rid of them now. They're poisoning your business, your customers and your other employees — and they're still doing it at this very moment while you're reading this chapter. Take action right away. Your customers and other employees will probably applaud you for it.

For one of my clients, the worst thing in their business had a name — Harold. He was their inside accountant. The founders of this property management company hired Harold because they were, like many entrepreneurs, a little disorganized and felt Harold would bring some order to their small company. Harold arrived and began organizing everything. He installed new and complicated computer programs to replace the old, simpler ones. He produced voluminous reports on financial aspects of the company. He drew up organization charts and wrote job descriptions for all employees. He held daily staff meetings for the eight employees of the company. One partner remarked, "We have more meetings than General Motors." The partners complained to Harold their profits were down because their staff expenses were up. Harold testily replied, "That's not my problem. See, it's not even in my job description." Harold was soon rewriting his job description at another place of employment. After getting rid of him, the two owners dismantled the bureaucracy and increased profits. They had gotten rid of the worst thing in their business and lived happily ever after.

The key to success in business is to stay focused on opportunities. It's hard to think about opportunities when you're spending all day dealing with problems. Start getting rid of your problems so you'll have more time for opportunities.

Let's Have a Pretend
Recession — Right Now!

A t the time this chapter is being written, business conditions are very good. Too good. Factories are selling all the new cars they can make. Car dealers won't make deals on popular models — they don't have to. Companies all over are having trouble finding good people to fill job openings. There are people working as independent contractors who, based on their skills, should be still flipping burgers at some fast food joint. Experts are saying we'll have clear sailing for at least the next 18 months. (Have you ever known these people to forecast a recession until we're already six months into it?) Certain magazines are saying that because of the global nature of the new economy we may not have a slowdown for 10 more years. Baloney! The pendulum will swing the other way — it always does — and it won't wait for a decade either.

When is the next recession coming? Who knows? My dad used to know. He worked as a freight conductor for the Pennsylvania Railroad. He could predict recessions by counting outbound and inbound box-cars from the industrial sidings he serviced. In the '50s and '60s, his predictions had uncanny accuracy. Today fewer companies ship by rail and shipping records don't reflect the output of service businesses that have become an ever-increasing component of our economy. I can't really tell you when the next recession is coming. But I can tell you how to handle it.

When times get good for too long, people get sloppy at running their businesses. That sloppiness gets them in trouble when times get bad. Perhaps the smartest thing you can do for your own business is to pre-tend that we're having a recession right now — it will keep you from getting sloppy. Here are four things you'd be doing during a recession that you should do right now:

Get rid of your slowest paying customers and clients. If they're having trouble paying you when times are good, do you honestly expect them to get better when the economy goes in the tank? Tighten up your credit and improve your collections now while times are good. If you don't take credit cards, consider changing that policy now. At the moment, banks are anxious to set up new Visa and Mastercard merchants; they'll revert to their more conservative posture when the recession starts. People use credit cards for almost everything — shopping, dining, buying gas for their cars and paying medical bills. With the advent of more business credit cards, more and more companies are using credit cards for business purchases, too.

Fire your worst employees, as recommended in Chapter 11. You're going to get rid of them anyway when times get bad, so why wait? Deal with employee problems the same way you deal with other things that displease you. No one ever says, "I really hate this restaurant. The food is half-spoiled and the service is terrible. As soon as the recession comes and I'm dining out less, I'll stop eating here!" If you've got half-spoiled employees who give you poor service, get rid of them now.

Hire only the best people to work in your business. You carefully screen your new hires when times are bad — there are a lot of good ones to choose from and you have extra time since business is slow. Be choosy during good times, too. You may have to set up evening or Saturday interviews — the good people already have jobs and they're not going to take time off work just to come in and see you. You'll have to sell them on your company — good people don't just change jobs for money — they want better working conditions and a positive career path.

Fourth, sell harder. You will anyway when times get bad. Start now. Clean up the store. Work the phones. Make more key contacts in your business world. Run ads and specials. Get out there and sell! Attract new customers and clients.

In the early 1980s, the Pacific Northwest was in a big slump. In my small manufacturing company's 1982 business plan, written in the fall of 1981, we said, "Of last year's top 20 customers, 10 of them bought less than $500 this year. Despite this, our sales increased by 75 percent during the period." Why? Because, frankly, we couldn't afford to have a recession. It would have sunk us. So we tightened our collections, fired the worst, hired the best, and sold hard. It worked!

If you'll have a "pretend" recession right now, you'll go into the real recession (when it comes) with the best customers and the best staff. Your customer base will be loyal and growing. Your business will continue to prosper and, who knows, you may not even realize there's a recession out there!

CHAPTER

1 3

Home-Based Businesses Shouldn't be Homely or Home-Like!

With all of the recent media hype about home-based business, you'd think it was some ground-breaking scientific discovery like finding a couple of extra planets in our solar system. It's not. Home-based businesses aren't new. In the 18th century, many of the small trade shops in the civilized world were home-based. In colonial America, many people had their businesses on the first floor in the front room of their homes. Betsy Ross did contract sewing in her home in Philadelphia. She created the first American flag while operating her home-based business. Later, during the Industrial Revolution of the 19th century, many of these cottage industries evolved into factories employing dozens or even hundreds of workers. These large factories became possible when the development and growth of railroads permitted economical shipping of merchandise made in one town to a destination hundreds of miles away. Technological change such as this fostered social and industrial change. Factories offered efficiencies of scale not possible in a home setting. Cottage industries declined.

Now, late in the 20th century, technology is once again refolding and retailoring our social fabric. The advent of the Information Age has allowed many of us to bring our businesses into our homes. Several developments contribute to this trend. The introduction of low-cost communication hardware is certainly one of them. In the early '80s, basic fax machines cost over $3,000. Personal computers were almost unknown. Primitive machines, like the Tandy TRS-80, cost thousands of dollars and offered few features. Software was equally primitive and consisted mostly of simple games. Today's sophisticated and affordable computers permit people to work at home, manage a great deal of

43

information in their own machines, and send and receive faxes. They can also produce professional quality documents and reports at home. Reduced telecommunication costs have also encouraged the establishment of home-based businesses. The cost of making a long-distance call has steadily decreased in inflation-adjusted dollars over the past 15 years. This permits people to communicate with each other (even over long distances) quickly and at a low cost, whether the means of communication is by voice, by fax, or by e-mail. No longer must people work in a corporate office environment to obtain favorable telecommunication rates.

Changes in our social structure have also promoted the concept of working at home. Many parents prefer to work at home in order to have more flexible work-time and to spend more time with their young children. The downsizing of large corporations has left many mid-level managers without jobs in the corporate world and with a distaste for seeking similar work. They have a great deal of experience in their field and a large number of business contacts. Many of these corporate refugees have started their own businesses and work at home to save time and reduce their operating costs.

It is estimated there are almost 40 million home-based businesses in the U.S. Some are bonafide, licensed, full-time businesses. Others are part-time, moonlighting-type businesses, some of which will eventually grow into full-time businesses. Home-based business is the fastest growing segment of the small business market and the numbers are expected to increase substantially over the next few years. It is estimated that by the year 2000, there will be over 60 million SOHOs — Small Office / Home Office — firms in the U.S. All kinds of people operate home-based businesses including designers, architects, consultants, writers, desktop publishers, commercial artists, bookkeepers, photographers, sales agents, video producers, repair technicians, accountants, engineers — and countless others.

Despite this very profound and wondrous portrait of the home-based business explosion, many of these new businesses are doomed to failure. The reason is simple. Their emphasis is on "home-based" rather than on "business." The best way to be assured of success as a home-based business is to stop acting like one! Here are five ways to insure your home-based business will be taken seriously by your prospects, customers and suppliers:

Establish regular and normal business hours. Having set hours will give your company a professional image and will help you keep your sanity. People have called my office on Saturdays, Sundays, and evenings, which makes me think a lot less of any business that does this. The implication is either they can't conduct business during regular hours or their customers aren't important enough to call during business hours. A salesman who was trying to sell me something called my office at 12:15 P.M. (lunch time), 5:47 P.M. and 7:45 P.M. What was he doing or who was he calling at 10:30 A.M. or 2:15 P.M.? Separate your business from your personal life by establishing hours of operation for your business.

Remember that your phone is your face. My office is in a downtown office building. The reception area is my face as is my office decor, my appearance, demeanor and that of other people in the office. People get their initial impressions from the business face which you present. Tami White, an AT&T representative, says it succinctly, "If your phone isn't working well, your business isn't working well." You may live in a $500,000 home and be wearing the latest designer clothes but no one knows it when you're on the phone with them. They judge you by the sound of your answering machine and the background noise as you speak. Make sure your outgoing recorded message isn't scratchy or worn, or doesn't contain disturbing sounds like jackhammers in the background.

If you're going to use an answering machine, get a good one. Be sure to get a separate phone line and answering machine for your business. There's nothing more disconcerting to a prospect than, "Hi! This is the home of Hal and Donna and the world headquarters of Designs International, Incorporated." Make your business sound like a real business. If you decide to use an answering service instead of a machine, get one that sounds like a receptionist in your imaginary executive office. Don't let your children be your answering service, either. Even older kids still sound like kids and despite their good intentions, they seem to always mix up messages.

Many home-based businesses use phone-fax splitters to save money. It permits them to run their phone and fax machine off the same line. All of my "techie" friends swear that these splitters are models of reliability but I've personally experienced problems dealing with businesses who use these devices. There's nothing more annoying than to call someone and get an ear-splitting fax signal. Is that the first impression you want to make on your prospects? I hope not. Get a dedicated fax or fax/modem line.

Speaking of first impressions, don't try to have business conversations on the phone while your prospect or business associate is being sere-naded with background noises from a barking dog or a screaming baby. Find a quiet place in your home to work. If you've got a baby and it's screaming, let voice mail or your answering machine take your calls until you've taken care of the problem.

Another area to insure professional conduct is to keep your excuses businesslike. I once engaged a home-based graphic artist to create a newsletter masthead for a social club. He sent me a first sample of the work.

"Look's great," I said. "Can you reshade the right-hand corner with a heavier screen and send me camera-ready hard copy as well as a disk with the logo as an EPS graphic?" "Sure," he said. "When will it be ready?" He hesitated. "Well, tomorrow is my day caring for my son, Todd, so I can't do it then. And I've got to take the dog to the vet on Wednesday. Oh, I'll get to it sometime this week."

That's a lot more than I ever wanted to know! Interestingly, the graphic artist did a good job and asked me for referral work so I recommended him to a friend. My friend contacted him and mailed him the job to be quoted. The graphic artist never called my friend back. Maybe the dog ate the mail. Or maybe Todd did!

Have a professional attitude and position yourself accordingly. Let's talk about attitude. There's no reason to charge less because you work out of your home. Too many home-based businesses make this mistake. They take an almost apologetic approach, confessing that they run their business from their home and then telling prospects, "... but you should buy from me because I'm cheaper than someone who has an office." This is a terrible marketing tactic. By taking this approach, you imme-diately position yourself as an inferior business. There's an excellent book called *Positioning — The Battle For Your Mind* by Ries and Trout (see Chapter 44, Resources). Study this book before you decide to take an apologetic position. You'll be convinced that lower pricing is a mis-take. If you're good in your field, charge the going rate for the products or services you offer.

Finally, take some of the money you save by working at home and spend it on things to improve your professional image — good business cards, a killer newsletter, or classy literature. There is still a stigma attached to working from home in the minds of some business people. Dispel their doubts by being more professional than your office-based competitors. Too many home businesses have cheap-looking business cards. Too many of them have post office boxes. A post office box is the sign of a fly-by-night outfit. If you don't want to use your home address, rent drop space at one of the mail service houses. You'll then have a street address and a suite number, even if your suite is the size of a shoe box!

I once worked for Rohm and Haas Company, a publicly-traded chemical company with annual sales of over $4 billion dollars. They had manufacturing facilities worldwide and had a rather large engineering and manufacturing complex in Bristol, Pennsylvania. Heck, they practically *were* Bristol, Pennsylvania. All of their mail came to P.O. Box 219. Once, I tried to place a $300 order from a small company in Redlands, California. They refused to ship the order unless we sent a money order in advance because, they told me, "Any company that was a *real* company wouldn't be operating out of a post office box." 'Nuff said.

There are many fine, professional home-based businesses that are very successful. By taking the five steps listed above, you can become one of them.

Is Your Business
Really a Good Investment?

For most business owners, their company is their largest single investment. Most owners used a big percentage of their personal savings or took out second mortgages on their homes to purchase or start their business. What's amazing is that many of these owners, who will move savings accounts and Certificates of Deposit from one bank to another just to get another quarter percentage point in interest rate, never look at the rate of return generated by their biggest single investment — their business.

To calculate your return on investment, you need to know two things — your return and your investment. Let's look at return first. In the classical sense, return is your net profit before taxes. For small, owner-operated businesses, return is net profit before taxes plus the owner's salary minus the salary that would have to be paid to a professional manager who would replace the owner. This adjustment needs to be made because some owners take very high salaries while others take almost nothing out of the business. We need to recast the return figure to get an accurate number for the real earnings of the business. Let's say your business made $5,000 in profit last year and you took only $12,000 in salary. You would have had to pay a professional manager $50,000 to operate your business. Therefore, your business really lost $33,000 last year ($5,000 + $12,000 - $50,000 = $-33,000). Suppose your business made $25,000 in profit last year and you took $115,000 in salary, and you would have had to pay a professional manager $80,000 to run your business. In this case, your business really made a $70,000 profit last year ($25,000 + $115,000 - $80,000 = $70,000).

How much would a professional manager get to run a business like yours? It depends on the business. For a small retail store, it might be less than $30,000; for a multi-million dollar, high technology company, it might be over $100,000. Ask your banker, your business adviser or your accountant. They know enough about your specific business to give you a narrower range.

Now that we've looked at return, we need to look at investment. To me, investment usually represents Total Assets. In the Assets and Liabilities portion of your financial statement, you'll see Total Assets listed. That's what you should use. Some people have used Net Assets (Total Assets minus Total Liabilities) to calculate return, but that's more a measure of leverage or how much money you've borrowed. If you're a marginally profitable company but have borrowed a lot of money, you may have a very high RONA (Return On Net Assets) percentage. For example, if you own a business with $20,000 in Total Assets and you owe your bank and your suppliers $19,000, your Net Assets are only $1,000. Suppose your business made a profit of only $600 last year. Your annual Return On Total Assets (ROTA) is, therefore, only three percent ($600 profit divided by $20,000 Total Assets), but your annual Return On Net Assets (RONA) is 60 percent ($600 profit ÷ $1,000 Net Assets)! That 60 percent RONA will give you a false sense of comfort (Hey! I'm makin' 60 percent per year return on my money!) when you're really almost broke! We want to look at Return On Total Assets (ROTA). It's a more realistic gauge for most small businesses.

If you can get a one-year, federally-insured bank CD paying over six percent, why shouldn't you expect a far higher annual return from your uninsured and far riskier small business? You should. Big businesses that are uninsured but far more stable than your small business, return about 15 percent. The Standard and Poor's Stock Index of the 500 largest, publicly-held companies has returned over 15 percent per year over the last 15 years. Since 1925, it has returned over 10 percent per year. Look for returns (ROTAs) for your own business of much more than 15 percent. Twelve years ago, my then-small manufacturing business had a ROTA of over 20 percent. What's your ROTA? Go measure it!

What do you do if your ROTA isn't as good as it should be? Two things. Improve your profitability and make your assets work harder. Most business owners know lots of ways to increase profits. They think about profits (or lack of them) all the time. They don't think so much about making their business assets work better for them. Here are some ideas:

If you own a restaurant, buy used equipment for the kitchen. It's plentiful, economical and most kitchen equipment lasts a long time. Spend your money where your customers can see it — comfortable seating and nice decor.

Defer capital purchases for as long as you can. If you don't need it, don't buy it. Can you fix up that old truck and repaint it? Perhaps that will buy you a few more years of service before you have to replace it with a new or newer vehicle.

Buy a refurbished mannequin for your store at a cost of $180 instead of a new one for $500. Look at used cash registers before you buy a new one. People come into your store because you have good merchandise, enticing decor, or well-done ads, not because you have a new cash register!

Does somebody want to sell you an existing business? Do they want to sell out for cash? Better make sure the money you invest in buying them out gives you a good return on your purchase. Run those ROTA numbers before you buy.

Before you buy a piece of equipment for $10,000, calculate the payback on it. How soon can it generate $10,000 worth of gross profit? Two months? Buy it! Two years? Forget it! One year? Maybe.

Machinery salespeople used to call on our business trying to sell us a numerically-controlled router. "You better get one," they said, "All of your competitors have one." We certainly did a lot of routed shapes — 53,000 per year. But given our efficient labor force and the $150,000 router cost, we couldn't justify it as a purchase — the numbers just didn't work out. The folks who bought our business now have a numerically-controlled router but they're doing more than twice as much volume as we were and they acquired a used one! If you can't justify it, don't buy it!

Make a rule starting today — don't buy any more assets unless you can put them to work in your business immediately and they pay for themselves quickly. Improve your return on your assets. Set a goal of 20 percent per year within two years and work toward it. Your business will improve and you'll be making your business far more attractive and valuable to a prospective purchaser should you ever decide to sell it.

Putting the Thrill
Back in Your Business

Remember when you first started in your business? Remember how excited you were? You used to get there early and clean everything in sight to make sure it sparkled and shined. You answered the phone with enthusiasm and excitement. The phone didn't ring very often and you wanted every caller to feel important. You made outrageous promises and delivered on them — even if you had to work Saturdays and Sundays to fulfill your commitments. Your business grew and prospered.

Now let's fast forward to today. You've got your business activities timed to the second. "If I leave the house at 8:15 A.M., I can get there by opening time." Clean everything in sight? "Hey, we've got a cleaning service for that." Displays and decor? "Call the decorating service." Ringing phones? "Just what I need. Another interruption. I'll just let it ring and Janice will get it. She knows how to get rid of them." Promises made, kept, and delivered? "No. We can't do that kind of thing in that short of a time period." "It's not our policy." "Our standard procedure is ... lemme see ... it's here in the book somewhere. Hey, pal, you don't understand how we work here ..." Your business isn't growing the way it used to and you're bored and frustrated. "Ya know, this thing isn't fun anymore. What happened here?"

What happened is the same thing that happens with other aspects of our lives. Routine. Taking things for granted, inertia, reduced expectations. Assuming everything will keep going along just fine even if we mentally set ourselves on cruise control. Acceptance of lower standards. These things will act just like termites, gnawing away at the very foundations of your business until it collapses. You've seen this happen to others; don't let it happen to you.

Here's what you should do. Pick out the most fun thing you like to do in your business. If you've delegated it away, take it back. If it's fun, you'll be good at it. So you should do it. Now pick out the thing in your business you hate to do. If you can, delegate it. Pick someone who's good at it and give it to them. Let them know the ground rules and your expectations. Then let them have at it. If it's something you can't delegate, pick a specific time to do it and get it done. Then move on to more pleasant tasks.

Look at your business with a new perspective. Is it doing what you wanted it to do? If not, change it even if that means restructuring or reinventing the business. Your business survived and became successful because it was a reflection of your personal values — your ideas about how things should be done, how customers should be treated, and how services should be offered. In the daily hustle and bustle of business tasks, have you forgotten your goals and values? Let's get back to those basic personal values that made you successful in the first place. Communicate your values to your staff and make sure that *your* business values become *their* values, too.

The 1970s were the start of the Marriage-Encounter movement. Couples with basically good but ho-hum marriages were urged to make a weekend retreat together to review their values. During that weekend they would rediscover each other, renew the feelings they had for one another when they first started out, and put the thrill back into their relationship.

Promise yourself that you'll sit down today and look at your business with fresh eyes, just as you did when you first started out. Put the thrill back into your business. You'll be happier and so will your customers and your employees.

S E C T I O N

I I I

Marketing

Marketing is the function that determines what the meetable needs of the marketplace are and, using this information, selects and/or designs the specific products or services to meet the needs of prospective customers. This definition of marketing has three important elements:

Meetable Needs: Everyone wants a filet mignon dinner for $1. That's a market need but you can't meet it and stay in business. A meetable need means it is a need that is not only technically feasible to meet but can be met realistically and profitably in a timely manner.

Selects and/or Designs: As the owner of a business and controller of your destiny you can modify your product or service to meet specific customer requirements. A salesperson for a Ford dealer can't produce a Ford Escort with a big Lincoln engine, a sporty Mustang interior, and four-wheel drive from a Ford Explorer. He or she is only allowed to sell what Ford offers.

Needs of Prospective Customers: You must run your business to please prospective customers. That is your primary purpose. Note that the definition does not say you must please your friends, your family, people you'd like to impress, your chamber of commerce, your post office, your church, or the world in general. Those are, at best, secondary goals. If you don't please your prospects by meeting their needs, you won't get any customers.

Marketing means planning to produce a cake that's within your cake-baking capabilities (on your first time out, stay away from a six-tier

53

wedding cake), and which people will want to eat (don't make a garlic cake with broccoli icing).

If you do your marketing right, you'll have a much easier time selling your goods, services, or cake!

Eleven Questions
Asked by the Experts

Marketing is an inexact science. Most people think of someone in marketing as a friendly, back-slapping kind of person. Nothing could be further from the truth. Marketing is an analytical game — an intellectual exercise. People who are marketing experts don't have to be glad-handing sales types. In fact, they may be introverted, anti-social, and be failures in the world of sales. It's their brain — their analytical skills — that's important, not their social skills. Good marketing people can analyze information such as buying patterns, sales trends, demographics, and competitive market share data. They can take this information and put together a logical, cohesive, and reliable marketing and sales plan.

In your business, you probably wear the marketing manager and sales manager hat. The important thing is to recognize which one you're wearing at any given time. You can be a great marketing manager as long as you can answer the 11 key questions about your company that any true marketing expert would ask. These questions are:

1. Who am I?

What are the capabilities and limitations of your company? Copy shops are outstanding at printing copies quickly. They are not printers of four color magazines. They can't produce hundreds of thousands of catalogs economically. They need to focus their attention on the segment of the printing market that needs 10 to 1,000 copies of documents produced quickly.

Another way to deal with this question is to ask "What am I good at?" "What am I dumb at?" Many graphic artists produce brochures, sign layouts, and line art. One graphic artist of my acquaintance only does logos. He says that it's what he does best. When our plastics business first started, we specialized in one-of-a-kind items — custom display cases for museums, special research tanks, and vessels for scientific studies, one-off prototypes for designers. As our company grew we moved away from one-off work and took on more jobs where 500, 1,000, or more pieces were required. Unbeknownst to me, our employees had lost the ability to make one good part. They knew how to make 500 — they'd make 510 and throw the first 10 pieces away because they were learning and machine set-up pieces. One day, while opening the top lid of our dumpster, we found nine museum cases inside. We had taken an order for a one-off custom job. My employees knew that we would be angry if they didn't make one that was good enough, so they made 10. They picked the best one to show to me and threw the other nine away. This might have been OK if the museum market was profitable enough so we could afford to throw out 90 percent of our work. It wasn't and we couldn't. My company was very good at making 500 of something but had become dumb at making *one* of anything. We either had to re-learn to do one-offs or abandon the one-off market. We chose the latter.

You can't fit in a market until you learn who you are. Then you'll know whether you belong in a particular market.

2. Who Are My Customers and Prospects?

Who makes up your target market? Where are they located? Many people make the mistake of defining their product or service and then stopping. You can't stop there. You have to figure out who is going to buy this product. If you don't do this, you may never be able to reach them and sell to them.

Several years ago, Gerber launched a new product. Gerber knew eating baby food was a secret vice shared by young parents. Sure, the parents made sure their toddlers ate the pureed spinach but the desserts, well, the parents themselves nibbled at the puddings, applesauce, and other tasty items. Gerber introduced a line of large, single-serving jars called Singles. It bombed. Here's why. Gerber thought it would be an ideal product for young single adults — an alternative to TV dinners and other single-serving entrees. The problem was that single adults don't remember what baby food tastes like. They won't find out until they become parents. New parents stayed away from Singles, too, because of the name and because eating baby food is a secret vice and they didn't want to let the *secret* out. Gerber never asked themselves who their customers were.

In the '50s, Alcoa hired an industrial designer to come up with a line of stylish, aluminum burial caskets. Most caskets are made of steel. Alcoa wanted a share of this 100+ million pound market. The designer came up with some elegant designs that took advantage of aluminum's unique fabrication properties — these designs couldn't be duplicated in steel. They introduced these new designs to the funeral industry and were met with (if you'll pardon the expression) dead silence. The funeral industry is a closed, tradition-bound industry. Funeral directors don't take well to new designs. Alcoa forgot that the family of the deceased is *not* their customer — the funeral director is.

The geographic location of your customers is important, too. If you own a flower shop in Boston, don't expect to get many customers from New York City. On the other hand, if you're a parking lot sweeping service in Gary, Indiana, there's nothing to stop you from pitching prospective customers in Chicago. The customers don't care where you're located since you come to them to do business.

When you figure out who you're customers really are, then you can tailor your product or service to be appealing to them.

3. Who Else is Like Me?

You've got to know who you're competing against. If you don't, how can you position yourself in the marketplace? You can't. It always makes me crazy when a business owner says, "Well, I really don't have any competitors because there's really no one quite like me." Baloney! If your business disappeared off the face of the earth tomorrow, where would your customers spend their money that they're now spending with you? Whatever the answer is — that's your competition. If Disneyland disappeared tomorrow, where would California vacationers spend their time and money? Perhaps Magic Mountain, Universal Studios, or Knott's Berry Farm. These are Disney's competitors. If Coke was taken off the market forever, would we stop drinking sweet drinks out of bottles and cans? Of course not. We'd switch to Pepsi, Dr. Pepper, or Snapple. If you're a CPA who rides a unicycle while doing general ledger trial balances and you're also a practicing attorney, what will your clients do if you ride your unicycle off a 2,000 foot cliff? Go to your funeral, hire another accountant, and find a new lawyer.

Your products, services and/or prices must be relatively attractive to get new customers and clients. Relative to what? Your competitors, of course. You can't devise a marketing strategy unless you compare yourself to and position yourself against a competitor of some kind.

4. What Do My Customers Need Now?

You don't have a business unless you've got a product or service which fills recognized needs of prospective customers. Notice the term "recognized." That means the prospect has to acknowledge and agree they need what you have to offer. Virtually all start-up businesses need one-on-one help and advice. Consultants and accountants have been frustrated in trying to sell them one-on-one professional help. The reason is that most start-ups have an "I've investigated this; I've researched this; I've read about this; now I know everything" attitude. These start-up businesses may need help and may be greatly benefited by it, but most won't acknowledge that they need it; therefore, they won't pay for it.

Small businesses need help in selling their products and services. Brochures and videos can be great sales tools. Most small business owners won't pay $10,000 to get a really effective video or four color brochure. They have a blind spot here and won't buy the talents needed to make knock-out sales tools. They may, however, buy them five years later and say, "I wish I had done this five years ago."

5. What Do My Customers Need Next Year? Five Years from Now?

By answering these questions now, you'll know whether you have a lasting market or not. You'll find out whether your market is real or a fad.

In the late '70s disco was big. So were disco dance floors. Every Holiday Inn and Ramada Inn in America seemed to have one. The floors were lit with flashing lights from below and were made from ¾-inch thick white translucent Plexiglas. Now white translucent Plexiglas is used for outdoor signs and light fixtures but in much thinner gauges. The only known use for thick, white Plexiglas is disco dance floors. In the '70s, specialty contractors sprung up specializing in the design, production and installation of disco dance floors. Such businesses were real money machines. Then, almost overnight, disco died. Most of those contractors never saw it coming. No wonder. They were so deep inside the tree trunks that they couldn't see that the forest was burning down.

It's OK to respond to a fad market as long as you have a profitable exit plan. In the early '80s, many supermarkets began to carry food and related items in bulk form. Flour, Tootsie Rolls, gourmet coffee, peanuts, laundry detergent, even dog biscuits were all served up in barrels and bins to be scooped out and bagged by the consumer. Most of the bins were made of clear Plexiglas; the barrels all had see-through acrylic plastic lids. Our plastic fabrication company jumped into the bulk food bin business. Stores would tell us what sizes and quantities they'd want and we'd make them. It was a very profitable business segment for our small manufacturing company. Then the business got more complicated. Stores wanted turnkey packages — stock bin designs supplied with metal racks, scoops, scales, barrels — everything. We had to decide if we wanted to make the considerable investment — in development dollars and inventory dollars to service the turnkey bulk food system market. We decided not to.

We had talked to enough people in the food business to know that there was a real concern about sanitary issues. The nature of bulk dispensing meant people could have direct contact with the food product itself. We felt there was a real possibility that a major tragic event would occur that would create negative publicity for the whole concept of bulk food dispensing and make the market disappear overnight. So we pocketed our profits and abandoned the bulk food business. Many of our competitors stayed in and increased their commitment to and investment in the bulk food bin market.

The bulk food fad didn't end with a bang; it went out with a whimper. Supermarkets have a defined and limited layout. Their square footage is fixed; therefore, when something new is installed something else is thrown out. Suddenly, salad bars in supermarkets became fashionable. Where to put them? Throw out the bulk food department! Ironically, the serve-yourself salad bar is as conceptually unsanitary as were bulk food bins. What about our bulk food bin competitors? Many of them went out of business. Others survived but struggled. We were glad that we exited when we did.

Today you can get a cafe mocha with whipped cream just about any-where. Seven years ago you couldn't have found such a thing outside of Seattle. Now there's a cart on every street corner and a little store in every strip mall selling expressos, lattes, and cappuccinos. Will they be around five years from now? Who knows? The coffee cart concept has all the makings of a fad. Will people abandon their $2.00 per day latte habit when the next recession comes and go back to drinking 50¢ cups of coffee? Sounds possible.

Of course, people have been drinking expresso and cappuccino in Europe for years now. It's not a fad over there. Fads never completely disappear. Expresso has been served in America for over 80 years. It was a big item in coffee houses during the '50s. People sipped it while lis-tening to beatniks read poetry. Light-up dance floors go back to Fred Astaire and Ginger Rogers. Bulk food has been and still is a staple at health food stores and alternative groceries. The problem with fads is that, when they fade, there's often not enough market left to provide you with a decent living.

6. Where Else Do Prospects Buy Now? Why?

Hopefully, you already know what and where your prospects are cur-rently buying. You need to explore this further by asking, "Why do they buy there?" Is it price? Service? Convenience? Inertia? You must know the answer in order to position your business in the marketplace. You can find out by asking six questions. These questions must be addressed to current customers of your competitors. You need to get out there and interview people either formally or informally because you must answer these questions in order to succeed. The six questions are:

1. What do you like most about where you buy now?
2. What do you like least about where you buy now?
3. What do you now pay?
4. Will you pay me more? Or less?
5. What do I need to do to get you to switch your business to me?
6. If I do these things, how fast will you switch your business to me?

Once you've answered these questions, you'll know your place in the business world and can devise a complete marketing and sales strategy.

7. What's My Line Area?

How many times have you been to a mediocre restaurant with undistinguished paintings for sale on the wall and a shoddy gift shop? This is a business whose owner doesn't know what he or she wants to be. One minute, a restaurateur. The next minute, an art gallery owner. Then, a gift store owner. The problem is the owner will never become an expert at any one thing. This owner needs to focus on a *single* line area, not three. If the owner had concentrated on the restaurant business instead of getting sidetracked, he or she might now be the proprietor of a *great* eating establishment. Decide what your line area really is. Then pursue it with a passion and a vengeance!

8. What's My Realistic Geographic Area?

Will people in Des Moines, Iowa travel to Minneapolis just to go grocery shopping? Hardly. Can a machine shop in Rhode Island solicit business from an aerospace company in California? Yes, if they can give that California company a reason to buy. Before it's eaten, 90 percent of all take-out pizza travels less than two miles. Most people won't travel more than 25 minutes by car when dining out at a fancy restaurant. That driving time is equally applicable, it seems, for choosing a dentist, doctor, barber, or hair dresser. Most travel agencies have clients in one or two zip codes — their own and, maybe, the one nearest theirs. CPAs rarely cross state lines; most only operate in one city or town. Attorneys are more prone to operate in more than one state — especially if their office is in a city near the state line. Lots of wholesalers and manufacturers on the West Coast ship up and down Interstate 5, between San Diego, California, and Bellingham, Washington because the shipping rates are low. Not many of them will venture that many miles eastward because the West to East shipping rates are considerably higher than North to South.

In your business, you need to define what your realistic geographic area is so that you can limit your advertising, promotional and sales efforts to that defined area.

9. What is My Major Competitor's Strength? Weakness?

In order for you to market your product effectively, you must know where your competitor is strong. Then you can market your product to minimize your competitor's strong points. You also need to find out where your competitor is weak. Your marketing efforts need to exploit your competitor's weakness, too.

In the automobile business in the '50s, the annual model change was a sacred ritual. Woe betide the brand that didn't update its look by rearranging chrome trim and resculpting steel panels. Volkswagen didn't keep the Beetle unchanged because they thought it was a wonderful design. They simply didn't have the money or the engineers needed to restyle their cars every year. Volkswagen exploited this weakness by running ads touting the resale value of their cars. Last year's Beetle looked just like this year's Beetle, so it didn't *look* like a used car — therefore, it held its value better than American used cars. Volkswagen did more than just minimize their weakness — they turned it into a strong point. Smucker's Jam (With a name like Smucker's, it's *got* to be good!) minimized the unappealing family name by turning it into part of a catchy slogan that spoke volumes about taste and quality with a simple phrase.

McDonalds does many things well, but they fry their burgers. Burger King broils theirs. In a memorable ad campaign in the early '80s, Burger King emphasized the fact they broiled their burgers. Broiling is considered healthier than frying, so Burger King had McDonald's on the run; they had found their weakness and capitalized on it. Sadly, Burger King later abandoned this ad campaign; recent ads have been far less effective.

In our plastics business, we started offering a line of store fixtures. It was a small line — 100 or so items. Prospects and customers told us we needed to add to our line. They pointed out a plastic competitor who offered a big catalog with over 1,000 products in it. We grew our line until we had over 350 products but were told "the other guy still has a lot more stuff." We started asking our customers why they bought from us, and discovered it was because we shipped quickly. So, here's what we did. We added another 50 or so items to our catalog but made the illustrations bigger so the number of pages in our catalog doubled. On the front cover, we put in large type, We Ship Every Order Within 48 Hours. We minimized our weakness by fattening up our catalog. Customers thought we had doubled the number of items. The fast shipping commitment hammered at our competitor's Achilles' heel. We picked up big gains in market share at our competitor's expense. We minimized our own weakness and exploited our competitor's.

10. Is There Room in the Market for Me?

There's nothing worse than being the third hardware store in a two hardware store town. Or the fourth car manufacturer in a big three automotive marketplace.

It takes a population of 5,000 or so to support a sit-down pizza parlor. You can easily verify this. Get out your yellow pages and count the number of pizza joints. Don't include take-out only or take-and-bake places. Multiply the number by 5,000 and you'll be close to the population of the area served by your yellow page directory. This estimate doesn't work in college towns because the students partake of a disproportional amount of pizza. College towns seem to have a pizza place for every 2,000 residents.

You can develop these numbers for your business, too. By counting yellow page listings in various cities and using population data from Rand McNally's *Commercial Atlas and Marketing Guide* (see Chapter 44), you can see if there's room for your business. You can determine how many people it takes to support a bookkeeping service or auto repair shop or ice cream parlor. Then you can check to make sure that there aren't too many in your town. If there are, you may want to re-think your marketing strategy.

You don't have to use number of businesses to compare population statistics. You can use square feet of retail space (pace off the outside of your competitors' stores). Or use employee counts by counting cars in the parking lots of factories. The main thing is to get a feel for the market — is it overcrowded or ripe for the picking?

In 1989, Battle Ground, Washington had three pizza places in a town of about 3,300 people. By 1997, the population had almost doubled and the pizza restaurants had dwindled to two. If pizza is your business, don't plan on opening in Battle Ground for a long time. We're still quite full at the moment, thank you.

11. If I Change My Approach, How Will My Competitors Respond?

They will, you know. Try to imagine how they will react so you can prepare suitable countermeasures.

If you take the time and do the research needed to answer these 11 questions, you can formulate a powerful marketing program that will leave your competition in the dust.

The Price-Volume Curve Is Baloney!

Did you ever take Economics 101? If you did, you'll probably remember the price-volume curve. You know, as unit sales volume of a product increases, manufacturing costs go down. This produces a higher profit, which attracts new competitors who drive down the price while further increasing market expansion and, usually, market size. This is very true in well-developed national markets, where big corporations slug it out to get an incremental share of market. McDonalds serves more meals than the Olive Garden. General Motors sells more Chevrolets than Cadillacs. So if you're going to make high-volume, commodity items like refrigerators, automobiles, personal computers or plastic soda pop bottles, you'd better pay attention to that curve.

On the other hand, if you're a smaller business in a market full of niches, you can disregard the price-volume curve. It doesn't apply to you. In the real world, there are enough high-priced (and high profit) opportunities with reasonable volume for a small firm, in the upper right-hand corner of the price-volume curve (see Figure 17.1). This should be your goal — to find the niche or segment of the market that provides reasonably high volume combined with high selling prices. That translates to high profits. Look for business opportunities in the upper right-hand corner of the field. That's the most profitable kind. Here are some examples:

Convenience stores charge the highest prices in town for most items. A well-located convenience store will have high traffic counts, healthy sales, fat margins, and merchandise turnover that even a supermarket would envy. Compare this with a small market in an older section of town. They have a clientele of mostly retired seniors who are price-sensitive, finicky,

Figure 17.1: The Price-Volume Curve is Baloney!

The real world is made up of many transactions. Most follow the traditional price-volume curve but there is enough data-scatter to support a niche market (in the upper right-hand corner) of reasonable volume combined with high prices.

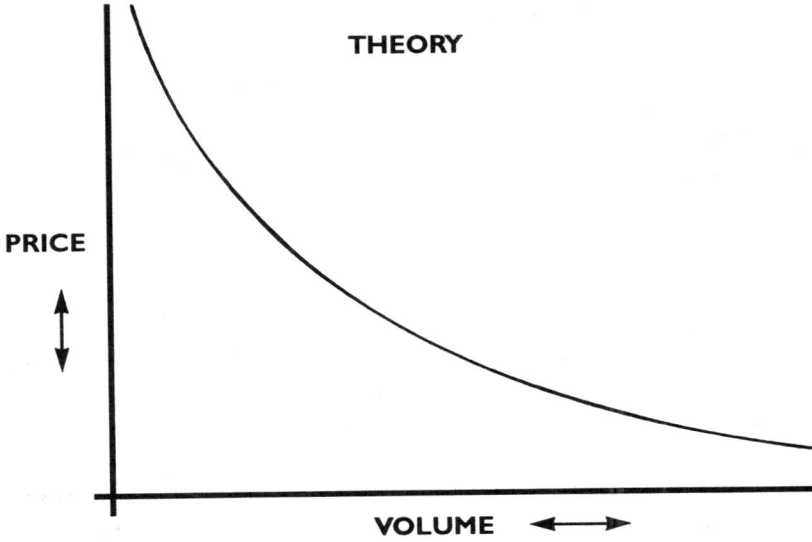

THEORY

PRICE

VOLUME ←→

Traditional Price-Volume Curve from Economics 101

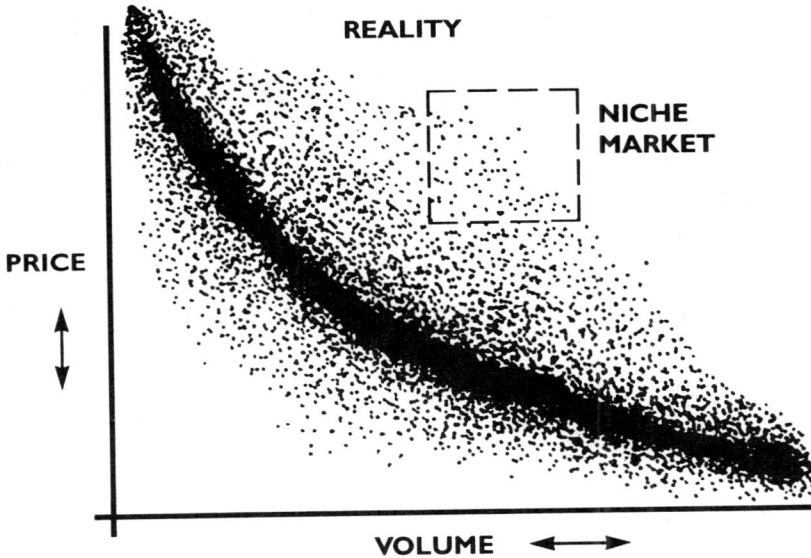

REALITY

NICHE MARKET

PRICE

VOLUME ←→

and who don't buy as much merchandise as a growing family does. The well-placed convenience store is a better bet than the old market, even though they stock mostly the same goods.

One of my clients came to me because they needed to improve profitability. After some initial inquiries, they were found to be the lowest-priced player in their market. On my recommendation, they raised their prices by 38 percent and they didn't lose a single customer. They took some 'of their newly-found profit and invested it in new production equipment. I advised them to take the rest of it and plow it into increased sales efforts. They did. They developed some point-of-sale materials that their customers used to generate more end-user sales for them. They moved their business from the lower left-hand corner of their business arena to the upper right-hand corner. Smart and profitable move.

Chapter 25 talks about the great disparity in pricing between various copy shops. Wouldn't you rather be a shop doing copies for ten cents each instead of two cents each? You can! Add value perception so you can move to the upper right-hand corner of the copy arena.

You've probably got a vinyl fabricator in your town. These are fairly low-margin businesses that make swimming pool liners or spa covers. In El Cajon, California, there's a company called Bigger Than Life, Inc. that fabricates giant inflatables from vinyl. They've made everything from Coke cans 20 feet tall to balloon figures for Macy's Thanksgiving Day Parade. They do over $5 million in annual sales and they're far more profitable than most ho-hum vinyl fabricators. Bigger Than Life, Inc. has found a profitable niche in the upper right-hand corner of the vinyl fabrication world.

Drug companies are typically billion dollar giants with multi-million dollar R&D budgets. Forest Laboratories is a smaller player that does almost no research and markets only generic and proprietary drugs. In 20 years they've grown from $5 million in sales to over $400 million with annual earnings of $100 million. They've found a home in the upper right-hand corner of the drug market.

In my display manufacturing business, department stores bought lots of clear plastic signholders. When they needed them, they wanted that shipment right away. Fast service was more important than cost. Restaurant supply houses used the same kinds of signholders. They bought less and were only willing to pay half as much as department stores. Why? Because a couple of my competitors were dumb enough to sell to them at low margins. Sports memorabilia distributors also bought signholders to display sports trading cards. They bought even less than restaurant supply houses. They bought from a supplier (now bankrupt and out of business) who was willing to make these holders at a price 40 percent lower than the restaurant supply houses paid. We didn't sell to the restaurant supply houses or the sports card distributors. We preferred to play in the upper right-hand corner of the market. Why didn't our competitors play there, too? Because they were so tired, exhausted, and broke that they didn't have the energy, resources, or the sales staff to explore new, more profitable business segments.

Many small business owners are too timid about raising prices. Hairdressers are always very worried about what another beauty shop down the street is charging. But grooming is a personal service and it's easy to create an upper-end niche by bundling other services into a total hair care package or by presenting a unique and upscale image with minor changes in decor.

We once produced vacuum-formed hemispheres for an amusement ride manufacturer. These orange and yellow domes were backlit and produced a colorful nighttime display for the ride. The company dictated prices. They were paying $10 per dome and were buying them from a vendor in Texas. They told us we had to match that price to get the business. We tooled up to produce them and struggled to make money. The domes were difficult to make. Our quality was much higher; our lead times were shorter and we delivered each shipment right to the customer's door. We decided that we weren't going to produce these hemispheres any more unless we could make a decent profit. So we raised our prices to $17 per dome. That was our "walk-away" price. We wouldn't make them for a penny less. We were nervous about such a large price jump but that's what we needed to make a reasonable return. Our customer screamed and yelled about a 70 percent increase but their alternative was to go back to their original vendor. By the time they paid freight from Texas and dealt with shipping damage problems, they were close to $17 anyway. We kept the business and moved this job from an unprofitable pain-in-the-neck to a profitable niche. Never be afraid to test price limits.

It's time for you to rethink your market. Where are you in your market arena? Is there enough business in the upper right-hand corner of your market to create a viable niche? What potential customers are in that upper right-hand corner? How can you reach them? How can you turn them into buyers? Find those profitable markets so you won't have to expend so much energy on selling to make a good profit. Remember, in the world of small business, profitable niche markets can make the difference between success and failure.

"Companies Like Yours Are a Dime a Dozen"

So here's the scenario — you worked late at your business last night, got home at 9:00 P.M., ate a quick dinner, and then started doing paperwork. Maybe you were doing quotes for customers, putting together an order for your store, or doing taxes. Before you know it, Letterman's almost over, so you go to bed and set the alarm for 5:30 A.M. Up early and rush off to work — you've got a million things to do before opening time. You're tired, overworked and then, sometime during the day, someone asks you, "Why should I do business with you? Companies like yours are a dime a dozen."

Sounds like fightin' words, right? Not necessarily. Sure you're angry because you're putting all your energy into your little business, but that person may have a point. Just because you're working long hours doesn't mean people ought to do business with you. You see, if someone thinks your business is the dime-a-dozen kind, it's because you haven't made a convincing case you have some significant benefits to offer to your prospect. To separate yourself from the pack of hungry competitors in your business world, you've got to do more than just work hard — you must differentiate yourself from everybody else.

To most people, tires are just things that are black and round. There are lots of different national brands but most people don't know what makes Goodyear different from Michelin. The tire dealers themselves all seem the same, too. Most have mediocre housekeeping and guys in dirty grey work clothes. Contrast this with Les Schwab. Schwab sells mostly private brand tires in Washington, Oregon, Idaho and Northern California but also offers the benefit of their slogan, "Sudden Service." It really is sudden. Employees hustle. And they're clean-cut and polite. The service bays are clean and well-lit. They get the work done quickly and get you on your way. Schwab has staked out a unique position in the tire marketplace and has left most other tire dealers looking like a bunch of dime-a-dozen guys. No one has successfully challenged Les Schwab.

Burgerville is a small company in the Pacific Northwest competing against the fast food giants. They've sent a fresh-not-frozen message to the marketplace that separates them from their competitors and brings in customers. They keep them coming back with innovative promotional and advertising programs.

Chef Horst Mager owned several restaurants in Portland, Oregon, including the Couch Street Fish House and The Rhinelander. Through continuing advertising and an effective public relations program, he convinced the buying public that if it's a restaurant owned by Horst Mager, it's going to give you a good dining experience. Horst separated himself from the rest of the restaurant pack. In fact, most of us don't even know who the rest of the pack is. I can't name the owners of any of the other upscale restaurants in the Portland area. Can you name any in your geographic area?

Those of you who remember the Bob Newhart show of the 1980s will surely remember Larry and the two Darrells. ("Hi. I'm Larry and this is my brother Darrell and my other brother Darrell.") On one show they presented Bob with business cards for their new business venture, Anything For $1.00. "We'll do anything for a buck," said spokesman Larry. Later in the show, Larry asked for their old business card back and gave Bob a new card. "We changed the name to Anything For $1.10," explained Larry. "We couldn't make any money doing stuff for only a dollar."

Make sure that you're not perceived as a Larry, Darrell and Darrell kind of business. Read Trout & Ries' book, *Positioning — The Battle For Your Mind*, for inspiration and ideas. It's listed in Chapter 44 of *this* book. Make sure you've positioned yourself so your customers and prospects know the unique and beneficial features of the products or services you offer. If you don't, they'll continue to think of you as one of those other dime-a-dozen businesses.

CHAPTER

19

Finding Gold
within the Mud and Silt

Any prospector worth his or her salt will tell you that when you pan for gold, you've got to go through a lot of mud and silt. There's some mud coming your way but it may contain hidden gold. No matter where you live, you'll be seeing changes over the next few years that will make your present business cards and letterhead obsolete. Area codes are changing and so are zip codes as regions of the country deal with continued growth.

What makes this situation muddy is that you're going to be dipping into your pockets to help make your favorite printer a little wealthier. A new area code or zip code means your business cards, invoices, letterhead, literature, and anything else with your address or phone number on it will have to be reprinted. You could just scratch out your old area code or zip code and write the new one over it, or buy some cheapie stickers to stick over it. But isn't that a little self-defeating? Didn't you spend all that money on good graphic design and printing in the first place because you wanted your stuff to look right? You knew first impressions are lasting impressions and you wanted to make the right impression on your prospects and customers. So don't mess it up; do it right.

While you're doing it right, maybe you should look at your overall image and see if you can update and improve it. Is your business card printed with burgundy ink on dusky rose paper and telling everybody that you haven't changed since you had those things printed in 1983? Or worse, is it brown ink on tan stock from 1975? By the way, do you still wear platform shoes and listen to disco music on those eight-track tapes? Is your logo a little old? Is it something that goes with that pink and charcoal boomerang Formica pattern from 1954? Do you remember "I like Ike"? If you fit in any of these categories, consider a redesign, and update. Call a graphic designer to help you. Since you're already reprinting everything anyway, it won't cost you much more and you'll get a whole new look. This is a real opportunity to change your image and that's the hidden gold in the mud.

What about your company name? Have you outgrown it? Do you need to modify it to reflect the changes in your business over the years? What do your customers call you? Federal Express renamed its service because everybody called it FedEx. How do you answer the phone? If your company name is Ace Roller Bearing Service and Distributing Company and you answer the phone "Ace Bearing," maybe it's time to rename yourself. Make your name more meaningful to your customers and clients. Another valuable opportunity previously obscured by silt and mud.

The inconvenience of these changes can be a golden opportunity for you. You can change your image, improve customer perception, tell prospects what you do in a more effective way and, maybe, put some extra gold in your pocket or purse. In 1995, I commissioned new business cards and stationery with contemporary graphics, new colors and changed the name of my business from the vague-sounding VIP Business Services, Inc. to Sherlock Strategies. I did this in 1995 when the phone company changed my area code. Why? Because I'm not a faceless company identified only by initials; I'm a one-man band named Sherlock helping businesses find and implement the right strategies for their success. My company name now reflects that. My stationery and business cards now look trendy and professional because I engaged a good designer to redo them.

Look at your business. Does its name and appearance reflect who you are and what you do? If it doesn't, maybe you shouldn't even wait for a new area code or zip code to prod you into a change. Maybe you need to do something about your image right now.

It's time to reinvent yourself and your company. Go for it!

CHAPTER

20

Lessons from Detroit (and Other Automotive Hot Spots)

Never in my career as a business adviser have I told a small company to go out and act like a Fortune 500 company. In fact, I've told most of my clients to take advantage of their company's smallness. They can provide far more personalized service than some big faceless corporation. Their small size makes them far more responsive to changing customer tastes than some giant bureaucracy. They are more nimble and can deliver goods and services faster than some huge mega-business.

Even though small companies shouldn't try to act like the giants, they would do well to study them and learn from the mistakes the big guys make. Best known of the biggies are the automotive companies — most of us are exposed to their products, advertising, selling, and customer service techniques almost every day. When groups of friends meet over coffee and their talk turns to discussions of consumer goods, they're not talking about dishwashers, T-shirts, sofas, or household detergents — they're most often talking about cars.

Cars represent everything that's American — good and bad. Automotive industry troubles, scandals and success stories are followed like soap operas. Lee Iacocca became the hero of the '80s, a celebrity, and a best-selling author after he saved Chrysler Corporation from oblivion. In universities throughout the world, professors use real-life car tales as examples in economics, marketing, and management classes. Ralph Nader gained fame by pointing out the shortcomings of the automobile companies. There are probably a thousand stories about the automotive industry — each story offers a moral and a lesson. These stories have become the Aesop's Fables of our Industrial Age.

In this chapter we'll look at 10 lessons from the automobile business — lessons you can apply to your own small business. These stories are relevant to your business even though you don't make cars or, perhaps, don't manufacture anything.

1. The Real Lesson of the Edsel

Edsel has become a noun used to describe something that bombed in the marketplace. Or someone who hasn't a clue. The Edsel was launched by Ford Motor Company as a 1958 model in the medium- or mid-priced field. Ford invested $350 million in the car and pulled it from the market in late 1959, citing poor sales. That's equivalent to about $2 billion in today's currency!

Many experts have claimed the problem with the Edsel was the name. It's certainly not a great name for an automobile but it's no worse as an abstract name than, say, Oldsmobile (a car for Old People?), Cadillac (an Indian Chief), Honda, or Nissan. People said, "Edsel sounds like pretzel." So what?! Honda rhymes with Rhonda. Ironically, Ford Motor Company even hired a poet, Marianne Moore, as a consultant to help pick a name for their new car brand. Her suggestions included Intelligent Bullet, Mongoose Civique, and Utopian Turtletop! Ford executives finally named the car after Henry Ford's only son, Edsel, who died in 1943. Edsel sounds a lot better than Utopian Turtletop! The problem with the Edsel wasn't the name.

Others in the automotive industry have said that Edsels had very poor quality, which drove customers away. To be sure Edsels had quality problems, as did most of the cars coming off the assembly lines at Ford, General Motors and Chrysler in 1958. No one ever named the '50s, "The Quality Decade." Edsels were made on the same assembly lines as Fords and Mercurys; their quality was about the same.

People have said the timing was bad for introducing the Edsel. That's certainly true. Henry Ford II himself said so in an interview shortly before his death. The so-called "Eisenhower Recession" began in 1957 and extended through 1958. It was not a good time to introduce a new product. Car sales in general were in a tailspin, but cars introduced in bad economic times will survive as long as the parent company has the capital and cash flow necessary to stay the course. Plymouth was launched just before the beginning of the Great Depression. Saturn was introduced just in time for the recession of 1990-91. Ford Motor Company certainly had the resources to stay the course with the Edsel, but they lacked the commitment to do so, and that's the rub.

Let's look at why the Edsel was developed. In the mid-'50s, Ford Motor Company had only one medium-priced car, Mercury. General Motors had three: Pontiac, Oldsmobile, and Buick. Chrysler had three — Dodge, DeSoto, and Chrysler. Ford wanted another brand to be less expensive than Mercury and compete directly with Dodge and Pontiac, which represented the lower end of the mid-priced spectrum. And so the Edsel was born.

The 1958 Edsel featured dramatic styling, a high performance V-8 engine, and distinctive technical innovations such as push button transmission controls on the steering wheel hub. The Edsel was a hot performer on the road and did respectably in the showroom, too. During the 1958 model year, 63,110 Edsels were produced. Edsel outsold DeSoto, Chrysler, and Studebaker. For every two Mercurys sold, one Edsel was sold. Not bad for a car in its first year of life, especially when you consider that Mercury was a well-established brand that had almost 20 years of brand loyalty and product history behind it.

In 1959, Edsel sales nosedived. Here's why. First, the distinctive styling was made blander. Second, the car was now offered with an economy six-cylinder engine as an option — hardly the way to bolster the car's performance image. The model line-up was substantially reduced. So were the number of dealers. The innovative push-button transmission controls were gone, replaced with the conventional column lever used in Fords. No wonder the car bombed.

All of these changes were made at the behest of Ford Group Vice-President, Robert McNamara, later U.S. Secretary of Defense during the Kennedy and Johnson Administrations. McNamara didn't like the Edsel. It looked too flashy, he thought, and it offended his sense of what an automobile should be — a no-nonsense, practical car. McNamara was a big fan of the bland and compact Ford Falcon, introduced about the same time the Edsel died. At the press preview dinner in 1957, before the Edsel had even been introduced to the public, McNamara told an associate, "I've got a plan for phasing it out." One automotive historian wrote that the Edsel would have survived if McNamara hadn't "axed it to bolster his ego."

In January 1958, McNamara disbanded the independent Edsel Division, folding it into the Lincoln-Mercury Division. Edsel dealers were soon told to get other franchises to represent, killing dealer enthusiasm, and support. In November of 1959, a few weeks after the introduction of the 1960 Edsel, production ended for good.

Many small businesses develop an idea, put time and energy into it, and then ignore it — letting it die a slow death. They cite the press of other business, or they say they've grown tired of it. The failure of the idea then becomes a self-fulfilling prophecy. If you're going to go to the trouble to develop a new product or service, be sure to give it the resources and time it needs to find its place in the market. Otherwise you'll have created your own Edsel.

2. The Rise and Fall of the People's Car

It sounds like the script for a Mel Brooks movie. Adolph Hitler orders a car for the German masses. The Nazi high command has it designed and prototyped. Hitler calls it the People's Car. Only a few examples are made before World War II begins. Germany loses the war. The tooling for the car is offered to Henry Ford II who laughs and turns it down, believing the car has no commercial future. Germans begin to assemble the car in the ruins of a bombed-out factory. The factory manager hires a Dutchman who knows little English to introduce the car to America. The design is now over 10 years old. The car looks strange and ugly by modern postwar standards. It is underpowered. It doesn't even have a gas gauge. It has lots of other little quirks including an ineffective heater. They don't even change the name — it's still called the People's Car. America falls in love with it anyway. It eventually breaks the long-standing sales record for a single model held by the legendary Ford Model T. For several years, there's a three-month waiting list to buy the little German car. The strange design remains basically unchanged for over 30 more years. Many of the quirks are still there 30 years later. People love the car anyway. As you may have guessed by now, the German word for People's Car is Volkswagen.

The success of the Volkswagen Beetle has been well documented. Yet today, the car company that took America by storm is a shadow of its former self. In 1962, four out of every five foreign-brand cars sold was a Volkswagen. Today, Volkswagen has a minuscule share of the U.S. market. For every VW sold today in the U.S., six Hondas and five Toyotas are sold. Even the newcomer automotive brand Hyundai outsells VW. What happened?

In the '50s, '60s, and early '70s, VW had a sterling reputation for quality. Their cars were well-made and the U.S. service organization stood behind the product. The warranty on the Beetle in the '60s was only 3,000 miles; yet, when my 1963 Beetle had excessive camshaft wear at 20,000+ miles it was replaced at no charge. The dealer said it shouldn't have worn that way and was obviously a factory defect. Volkswagen could afford to stand behind the product; it was a durable and well-crafted design. The workers had lots of practice in building the Beetle because they never changed it! Detroit changed its product every year and the workers were re-trained and the tools were debugged as they were building cars. Therefore, they made a lot more "lemons" than VW.

There was an apparent need, even in the late '50s, for a new VW model. The factory designed and built dozens of prototypes of proposed new models over the years but VW management was indecisive and wouldn't commit to production. Finally, in the '70s, faced with a declining market share worldwide, Volkswagen introduced the Rabbit. It was totally different from the air-cooled, rear-engined Beetle. The Rabbit had a water-cooled engine in front and front-wheel drive. The car was shorter and more space-efficient than the Beetle and was initially praised by the automotive press, but there were clouds on the horizon. The car had some inherent problems, apparently because the design and development was rushed to get the car to market. The engines wore quickly and burned oil excessively after only 30,000 miles in many cases. The overall quality wasn't nearly as good as the Beetle — paint and trim faded quickly, upholstery wore and tore after a short time. The dealer support network was pinching pennies and was far less willing to cover out-of-warranty claims for dissatisfied owners. The air conditioner compressor on my new 1976 front-engined VW fell out of the engine compartment. The factory claims center refused to cover the repair even though the car was only 300 miles out of warranty. Contrast this with the way VW handled problems 13 years before. Obviously there was a big change in attitude by the factory.

Finally, the industry standards had changed. No longer was the benchmark the early '60s Detroit iron; now the standard of automotive excellence was defined by the Japanese imports, which were very well-made indeed. During the '70s and early '80s, loyal owners of air-cooled VWs traded in their Beetles and Karmann Ghias for new Rabbits and Sciroccos. Many were disappointed with their new purchases and abandoned VW as a favored marque, moving to Toyotas, Hondas, Nissans, or newly improved American cars for their next purchase. Ultimately, VW's market share declined. In 1988 Volkswagen closed its plant in Pennsylvania that had opened in the late '70s to fill the North American demand for Rabbits.

The lesson here is that you've got to keep up with the times. Don't let your product or service become old hat. But, as you change with the times you must not abandon those virtues your customers love and expect. Volkswagen lost its virtues of quality and reliability and is now paying the price.

3. The Sinking of the Flagships

In the early '50s, Lincoln was a small player in the luxury car field. In 1951, Lincoln was in 18th place among car manufacturers, selling less than 33,000 cars in a model year while Cadillac sold over 110,000 automobiles and Packard moved more than 100,000 units. In the early '50s a Lincoln looked a lot like the lower-priced Mercury, and Lincoln was perceived by many as just a gussied-up Mercury. No one ever said that a Cadillac was a gussied-up Buick.

Lincoln needed a change and decided to develop and produce the ultimate luxury car — to become the flagship of the Lincoln luxury model line. The car, christened as the Continental Mark II was introduced to the world at the Paris Automobile Show in the fall of 1955. Debuting as a 1956 model, the Mark II was a handsome, conservatively-styled automobile. It was priced at about $10,000, which was about twice the price of a new Cadillac or *ordinary* Lincoln and about the same price as a Rolls Royce. Ford expected to sell 3,000 to 4,000 Mark IIs per year. It didn't happen. People who are prepared to spend that kind of money want the prestige of a foreign name — Rolls Royce or a Ferrari. The Mark II was discontinued in May of 1957 with only about 3,000 units produced in two model years.

You would think that the Continental Mark II experience would have stood as a lesson for other luxury car makers. Yet in 1957, Cadillac introduced *their* flagship, the Eldorado Brougham. This was a four-door super-luxury Cadillac priced at over $13,000. In a four-year period,

Cadillac sold less than 1,000 examples. In 1960, Cadillac cried, "Abandon ship!" and discontinued the Brougham.

If Cadillac didn't learn the lesson taught by the Continental Mark II, would it learn the lesson after the Eldorado Brougham fiasco? Nope. In 1987, Cadillac introduced the Allante, a high-priced two-seater sports car targeted at Mercedes Benz's line of sports cars. The bodies for the Allante were produced by Pininfarina in Italy, then flown via specially equipped Boeing 747 cargo planes to Detroit for final assembly and powertrain installation. (The cargo planes were called the Allante Airbridge.) The Allante's 1987 base price was $55,000. This is an interesting number, because the $10,000 price tag of the 1956 Continental Mark II was about $55,000 in 1987 dollars. Cadillac expected to sell 6,000 to 7,000 Allantes per year at that price. They were quite disappointed. The cars were discounted massively just to move them. My business partner, John, bought a red Allante in 1988 as his company car; we paid $34,000 for a never-titled demonstrator with 2,000 miles on it. Sales of the Allante varied between 600 to 3,000 per year. The Allante was quietly discontinued in 1993.

These stories provide two lessons. The first is — learn from the mistakes of others in your business world. Before you launch a new product, service, or program, study the market. Who else has tried this before? What were the results? Do you have any logical reason to believe that your results will be different? K.C. Truby, a well-known business speaker, says, "There are two kinds of people in this world. The first are those who learn from the mistakes of other people. The second are other people."

The second lesson is — perception is reality. No matter how good a car is, if it's built by Detroit, it will never carry the prestige of a foreign car such as Mercedes, BMW, or Rolls Royce, at least not in the U.S. You're often an unsung hero in your own hometown (or home country). Make sure your business plans are firmly anchored to earth. You can't change perceptions overnight. Changing your image in the mind of the prospect takes years. If you're perceived as a discount store, your path to creating a more upscale image is a long and arduous one. If you're trying to create a flagship brand, don't overreach, or your flagship may sink!

4. Keep Trying Until Something Works

Where have you heard this phrase before?! This basic lesson, which was the title of Chapter 4, is applicable to the automotive industry, too.

In the late '50s, Datsun (Nissan) and Toyota made a run at the American market. Both companies failed. Their cars were small but heavy sedans with interiors that were uncomfortable and rough by American standards. These automobiles had engines and gearing suited for low-speed Japanese roads. When brought to California and driven on the freeway their powertrains were overtaxed and soon failed. Both came back to the American market again in the early '60s with more reliable but odd, uninspiring little cars. Their beginning dealer network consisted mostly of repair garages and used car lots who couldn't get a dealer franchise from any other automobile manufacturer. The cars themselves had shortcomings and people complained. The Japanese listened to complaints and acted quickly to fix them. The autos got better and better. Toyota and Datsun worked to improve their dealers, too. By the mid-'70s, both Datsun and Toyota were outselling Volkswagen. They kept trying, and improving, until they became major players in the U.S. car market.

Persistence pays. In the automotive industry and in your own business. Keep trying until something works, and then keep working to make it even better.

5. Dare to Be Different

Earlier, I mentioned that Lincoln used to be a minor player in the American luxury car field. In the '50s and '60s, they were outsold by Cadillac by a factor of 3 to 1, sometimes even 4 to 1. In the '70s, they made some gains against Cadillac having introduced their Mark III, IV and V series of two-door personal luxury coupes to compete with the two-door Cadillac Eldorado coupe, though Cadillac still outsold Lincoln by 2 to 1 or more.

In the mid-1970s, Cadillac introduced the Seville, a small luxury sedan that was based on the Chevrolet Nova platform. The Seville was well styled — it was attractive and looked nothing like the Nova. It sold very well — 40,000 to 50,000 units per year. The Seville remains in production today as Cadillac's smaller luxury sedan. It remains well-styled and still sells well, although it is no longer based on a Chevrolet platform. Lincoln responded to the Seville by hurriedly sticking a Lincoln grille and spare tire hump on a Ford Granada, christening it the Lincoln Versailles. The Versailles fooled no one and was discontinued in 1980, after selling only 50,000 cars in four years. Ironically, Cadillac learned nothing from observing the Versailles fiasco. In 1981, it introduced the

Cimarron which was a mildly restyled Chevrolet Cavalier sub-compact with a leather interior. It fooled no one either, never sold well and was withdrawn from the marketplace after a few years.

Lincoln, having learned its lesson, dared to be different. In the '70s and '80s, Lincoln made a conscious effort to improve the quality of its cars, while Cadillac's quality slipped. The front-wheel-drive Cadillacs developed annoying rattles as they aged; older Lincolns were still very quiet. Cadillac had some bad engine problems in the late '70s and early '80s, notably with the V-(8-6-4) engine and the diesel V-8 engines. Lincoln also offered optional diesel power for a few years but the engines used were proven, high quality six-cylinder motors imported from BMW. In a big cost cutting move, GM forced more of its car divisions to share more body components. Cadillacs, Buicks, Oldsmobiles, and Pontiacs were difficult to tell apart.

Lincoln capitalized on this in a famous, long-running television ad for the Lincoln Town Car featuring Cadillac, Buick, Oldsmobile, and Pontiac owners trying to tell their cars apart when delivered by a valet parking attendant. Interestingly, the Lincoln Town Car shared its basic platform with the big Ford and Mercury but it was cleverly styled so that it looked quite different from the Ford Crown Victoria or Mercury Grand Marquis. Lincoln had positioned itself to take advantage of Cadillac's distress and its move paid off. In 1988 and in early 1995 Lincoln actually outsold Cadillac and, while Cadillac has spent a lot of product development and advertising dollars to recoup market share since then, Lincoln's sales are usually very close to Cadillac's. That's a far better batting average than the old days and a big step forward for Lincoln.

The lesson here is to be prepared to differentiate yourself from your competition and be ready to exploit any new weaknesses which your competitors develop.

6. Focus on What's Important — Customers

Honda was a latecomer and upstart in the Japanese car market. Toyota and Nissan (Datsun) had been making cars since the 1930s. Honda began life in 1949, producing small stationary engines and motorbikes. Honda grew to become the world's largest motorcycle manufacturer and offered its first car for sale in 1962. It was a very small car, not exported, and not well-suited for American use. Honda watched and learned from the mistakes of

Nissan and Toyota as they struggled to become successful in the U.S. market in the early '60s. In 1972, Honda offered the Civic, a car acceptable to Americans and very competitive with the VW Beetle. When the first gas crisis arrived in the U.S. in 1973, Honda was well-positioned to take advantage of the sudden demand for small economical cars. Sales of the little, economical Civic skyrocketed. By 1975, Honda was selling 100,000 Civics per year in the U.S. In 1976, Honda offered a slightly larger car, the Accord, first as a two-door coupe, later as a four-door sedan. The Accord was a big hit and, when the second gas crunch occurred in 1979, Honda became so popular that there was a long waiting list for prospective Honda buyers. One automotive writer described the 1980 Honda Accord four-door sedan as a little Mercedes Benz at one-fifth of the Mercedes price. The Accord offered economy and value in a package size suitable for American buyers. Honda was the first Japanese manufacturer to produce cars in the U.S.; it opened a plant in Marysville, Ohio in 1982 to produce Civics and Accords and became the best-selling Japanese brand in the U.S. Honda was the first of the Japanese manufacturers to offer a luxury car to U.S. buyers — the Acura Legend.

Honda has succeeded because they focus on what's important to prospects and customers. They had great initial acceptance in the U.S. because their cars were styled more to American tastes. They didn't look as "Japanese" as Toyotas and Nissans did. Honda is a very innovative company in technical matters but they focus only on those matters that have practical importance to the customer who buys their car. Their CVCC engine of the mid-'70s was a technical marvel but the main advantage was it could burn gas efficiently with less emissions. The engine needed less restrictive pollution control equipment, which would hinder its performance and efficiency. This benefited the consumer with a better balance of gas mileage and performance.

Despite the day-to-day trivia and tasks involved in manufacturing, promoting, distributing, and selling cars, Honda has focused on what is important — the needs of prospective customers. You should too.

7. Killed by Family Members

The first DeSoto was introduced in 1928 by Chrysler Corporation as a less costly alternative to a Chrysler. In the 1930s, if you didn't have much money, you'd buy a Plymouth. If you wanted something a little better, you'd buy a Dodge. If you had lots of money and wanted the best the company could offer, you'd buy a Chrysler. If you didn't quite have enough for a Chrysler but wanted something better than a Dodge, you'd buy a DeSoto. That's the way things remained until the early '50s. A DeSoto was a car built on a Chrysler chassis with fewer luxury touches. Then Chrysler spun off the Imperial as a separate model line. Imperial became the flagship luxury car; the Chrysler brand moved down a notch into the mid-price field. Meanwhile, Dodge was expanding its model line with more costly models at the top of its range. In 1940, DeSoto sales were about 70 percent of Chrysler sales. During the same model year, Dodge outsold DeSoto by 3 to 1. By 1960, Chrysler was outselling DeSoto by 3 to 1; Dodge was outselling DeSoto by 14 to 1! DeSoto was being squeezed from both ends — by Dodge on the lower end and by Chrysler on the upper end. DeSoto never had developed enough identity and market strength of its own so it was easily suffocated. The last model year for the DeSoto was 1961.

Here's the lesson: if you're making changes in your catalog of products or menu of services, watch out! The changes you make to one item may adversely affect something else you make or sell. If you try to be a restaurant and a dessert cafe, the dessert business may rob seating and patrons from your restaurant business. That's OK if you've planned for it and haven't depended on the revenues from the restaurant business to pay your overhead. If you did, you may be in trouble. Before you act, consider the consequences.

8. Raising the Club Initiation Fee

It used to be easy to get into the car business. In the first few decades of the 20th century, lots of entrepreneurs got into the automobile business. Fortunes were made and lost. As the industry went through a prolonged period of consolidation many of the early entrepreneurs sold out to larger car companies and spent the rest of their lives living off the proceeds. As the industry continued to mature, it became harder to break into the automobile manufacturing business. After World War II, several people tried to get into the automobile business but couldn't succeed because of the capital required to start and sustain an automobile manufacturing business. Mini-cars like the three-wheeled Davis or the golf cart-like King Midget came and went. So did sports cars like the Kurtis, Woodhill, and Muntz Jet. Luxury cars like the Gaylord and Tucker never made it either. By the '70s, increased government regulations meant it took a really big bankroll to get into the business. That didn't stop two entrepreneurs from trying.

Malcolm Bricklin was a Philadelphia-born businessman who wanted to be a car producer. Bricklin had been successful running a building supply business and importing Subaru automobiles. He developed the Bricklin SV-1, introduced in 1974. The car featured gullwing doors and a fiberglass plastic body with a weather-proof solid color Plexiglas exterior skin. The V-8 powered car had an engine from American Motors and was manufactured in New Brunswick Province in Eastern Canada for two years. Bricklin ran out of money and the company went bankrupt after producing about 2,800 cars at an investment cost of $30 million.

A few years later, John Z. DeLorean, a former General Motors executive, introduced a mid-engined sports car powered by a Volvo V-6 engine. Like the Bricklin, the DeLorean was named after its creator, had gull-wing doors, and used a fiberglass body with an impervious surface — this time a stainless steel exterior skin. Priced at $25,000 each, the DeLorean was produced in Northern Ireland from 1981 to 1982 but failed to make a profit. The company was placed in receivership and the assets liquidated. The DeLorean was consigned to the minutiae of auto-motive history after spending an estimated $200 million and producing 8,400 cars.

The lesson of DeLorean and Bricklin is that you can't be a successful car manufacturer today unless you've got a great deal of capital to invest. How much? Obviously $200 million isn't enough. The consolidation of the automotive industry and the increased government mandates regard-ing safety, emissions, and other compliance testing means the initiation fee to join the club has become very high indeed. As a small business owner, anything you can do in your trading market to slap a high initia-tion fee on new competitors will help you keep more of your market.

In my plastics display business we did several things. There are, by my estimation, about 1,100 active, full-time, acrylic plastic fabrication busi-nesses. Many are small operations with one or two employees. All were potential competitors. We started raising the initiation fee by developing a catalog of stock designs. Only about 50 of these companies were will-ing to make the investment in time and money to produce such a cata-log. We raised the initiation fee again by having several of our plastic items injection-molded. Tool-up costs for injection-molded parts were substantial and it added to the initiation fee. Finally, we kept virtually all of the items shown in our catalog in stock for immediate shipment. This required several hundred thousands of dollars investment in finished goods inventory and raised the initiation fee even further. We now had a unique place in the display market and were not easily challenged.

One of my clients produces replacement parts for paper industry equipment. They have a catalog and inventory and contacts within the industry. Even though the parts they produce are unpatented and could easily be produced by many machine shops, they have no competitors. It's just too hard for other machine shops to invest the time and money to develop the market knowledge, contacts, catalog, and inventory to address this market segment.

Make it tough for competitors to be in your market. Keep the dues high and raise the initiation fee. It helps keep out the riff-raff!

9. Mid-Life Identity Crises

The automotive market is constantly changing. Brands that lose their focus blur their identities and give up their market share.

Consider Oldsmobile. In the old days, Oldsmobile was a technically innovative producer of medium-priced cars. Oldsmobile offered the first production car with a chrome-plated radiator shell in the '20s. In the '30s, it was the first General Motors car to offer hydraulic brakes and an all-steel top. In 1940, Oldsmobile was the first major car line to offer a fully automatic transmission. In the '50s, there was Oldsmobile's high performance Rocket V-8 engine. In 1966, Oldsmobile offered the first American V-8 front-wheel drive car — the Toronado. Oldsmobile was more expensive than Pontiac plus it had a youthful image. Buick was comparably priced with Olds, but had a much more conservative approach to styling and engineering. Bankers bought Buicks; the real up-and-coming movers and shakers bought Oldsmobiles.

Then things began to change. In the late '50s, Pontiac began to reinvent itself as a high performance car. In the '60s it pushed that image further along with the introduction of the high-powered Pontiac GTO and, later, the sporty Firebird. It moved upscale with the luxurious Grand Prix and Bonneville lines. Pontiac was now encroaching on Oldsmobile's performance and price turf. Pontiac was also offering design and technical innovations that rivaled Oldsmobile's. Meanwhile, General Motors was busy consolidating and standardizing mechanical components for its various car lines and Oldsmobile lost even more of its edge in technical innovations.

By 1980 most Oldsmobiles shared engines, transmissions, suspensions and other mechanical components with other GM car lines. It took the public a little while to figure this out but, when they did, Oldsmobile's share of the mid-price market began to decline. During the late '50s, Oldsmobile outsold Pontiac by more than 20 percent. By the mid-'80s, Pontiac had caught up with Oldsmobile and began to surpass it. By 1992, Pontiac was outselling Oldsmobile by 42 percent. Oldsmobiles sales had dropped from over 800,000 units per year in the early '80s to less than 400,000 per year by the early '90s. What was GM's mid-price performance brand? Pontiac. What was GM's innovative brand? Who knows? Not Oldsmobile. Oldsmobile's image was blurry. It certainly wasn't a performance or innovative brand. It was just another car with an identity crisis.

Oldsmobile wasn't the only car to have its identity hijacked. During the '40s, '50s, and early '60s, Plymouth was part of the "low-priced three." Chevy was the top-selling brand of automobile in the U.S. Ford was usually a close second. Plymouth was a solid third. In the mid-'60s, Pontiac stole third place, bumping Plymouth to fourth. Then the imports came along and hurt Plymouth some more. Chrysler's quality and financial problems battered Plymouth even further.

As Chrysler reinvented itself in the early '80s, Dodge moved down into the low-priced field. Since Dodge had always been perceived as a medium-priced car, it was now perceived as a "classier" car than Plymouth. Dodge began stealing sales from Plymouth. By 1982, Dodge outsold Plymouth as a brand by a small margin. By 1993, Dodge was outselling Plymouth by a whopping 63 percent. In fact, Plymouth was outsold by every domestic make of car except Chrysler. Plymouth is having its own mid-life crisis. It needs a defined and focused identity in the marketplace. Chrysler is working to change this with the introduction of the heavily-promoted Plymouth Breeze and the sporty Plymouth Prowler hotrod but it will be a long haul to resurrect Plymouth's identity.

Both Oldsmobile and Plymouth are trying to compete in an overly crowded marketplace. Their problems are the same as faced by many small businesses in America. Most office supply and stationery stores never developed much of an identity. They were just there — somewhere in town. Now that big office products discounters such as Staples,

OfficeMax, and Biz Mart have come to town, the old line office supply stores have to re-invent themselves just to survive.

Fast copy shops such as Kinko's, Quikprint, PIP Printing, and Lazerquick have wrought havoc with small independent printers. Many of these small print shops never made a sales call. Now they must develop a marketing strategy and get out there every day and hustle for business or they'll die. They need to develop extra services that can't easily be matched by franchised copy shops. They must add local flavor and personal service to distinguish them from their cookie-cutter competition.

In the plastic distribution business, the big players get super-low prices by buying blocks of manufacturing capacity from their major suppliers. The very small players survive by offering faster service and by adding value, doing special cutting, shaping, or drilling to the plastic that they distribute. They've become specialists, serving particular niches of the marketplace. The mid-sized distributors are fighting for their lives. They can't get the pricing deals offered to the big guys and they don't have the nimbleness of the little guys. Many who failed to stake a unique position in the changing marketplace and whose fortunes crumbled, have been acquired by the mega-giants, who are always looking for new branch sites — at cheap acquisition prices.

In the cardboard box game, manufacturers of corrugated cartons have had to become problem-solvers for their customers, offering a broader line of packaging materials and fabrication services to differentiate themselves from hungry competitors. No longer can a box company simply offer a few stock carton sizes. They must provide a full range of products and services to their prospective customers.

What about you? Who are you? How do your customers perceive you? What needs are you filling in the marketplace? Who is your competition? If you can't answer those questions, you may find yourself in the same dilemma as Oldsmobile and Plymouth.

10. The Niche Market of Death

Before there were automobiles, there were hearses. They were pulled by a team of horses. As motor vehicles replaced horses, a few coachbuilders began producing a self-propelled hearse on a truck chassis. By the early '30s, hearses were being built using passenger automobiles as a starting point. These funeral coaches were made from several brands of automobiles, including Studebaker, Nash, Buick, Reo, Packard and Cadillac. After World War II, Cadillac and Packard dominated the hearse market. With Packard's demise, Cadillac easily became the dominant player in the funeral car market. Cadillac sells partially assembled cars to custom body manufacturers such as Superior and Miller-Meteor, that make them into hearses. The market is small — only 500 to 2,500 hearses are produced in a model year, but Cadillac reaps other benefits from being in this market. Many funeral directors like to have a matched set of vehicles, so they buy Cadillac sedans and limousines as well. Cadillac supports the funeral vehicle market by advertising in trade magazines, such as *American Funeral Director*, and by providing technical and marketing support for the hearse body builders. It's a small but profitable market niche and Cadillac has become the dominant player.

Many successful small business owners have profitable, unobvious niche markets. In the '80s, Hewlett-Packard used to provide free donuts and coffee to their employees in many locations. A small bakery shop had the donut contract for one of H-P's facilities. It made the difference between survival and failure for this tiny business. A manufacturer of industrial machinery has a very small and profitable sideline, making and selling parts for antique farm tractors. It is a very high margin business segment for them. An attorney of my acquaintance has specialized in product licensing in the entertainment industry. His expertise is unique and commands high prices in this niche.

Most graphic designers get $500 to $1,000 to develop a logo package for a business client. Right down the street from one such designer is a graphics company that charges $15,000 for the same service. They've specialized in two industry segments that will pay these kinds of prices. Their clients are obviously satisfied with the value delivered because they keep coming back with more work and referring their business friends. The $500 logo designer up the street doesn't even realize this market exists. He says he can't figure out how the other firm stays in business. He gets red-in-the-face when he sees them driving new and expensive cars, but he's spending his time fuming instead of looking for market segments where he can improve his margins.

As you deal with the day-to-day tasks of your business, be sure to keep your eyes and ears open for opportunities in obscure, unobvious market niches. A good niche can make you rich!

My First (and Probably Last) Restaurant Review

S ome time ago, I gave a talk to a business group. Afterward, a woman came up to me and said she owned a restaurant. "We really serve the best Mexican food in the area," she said. "But we're not making any money and I'd like to meet with you to see if you could use your consulting skills to help me." We agreed to meet later in the week at my office. I had never been to her restaurant, so I stopped by the next day for lunch. I took three pages of notes during lunch in preparation for our meeting. The woman never showed up for her appointment. Well, just because she stiffed me doesn't mean that my observations have no value. I'd like to share some of them with you because they have implications for your business, too, even if you're not running a restaurant.

For openers, the place looked dumpy from outside. The door had those slanted gold hardware store letters spelling out PULL, but the L had fallen off so it said PU L. Not a good first impression. The front windows were covered with those freebie signs that the beer companies give out, so the restaurant made no statement about itself (except that it served beer).

Walking inside, I saw that the place was decorated with a combination of promotional signs for soft drinks and garage-sale cast offs. The decor included junky Tijuana-style trinkets, bows, and hats. A newspaper had written a very nice restaurant review, which had been laminated and hung with rubber suction cups. It deserved to be matted and framed. The place could have used less hanging piñatas and more hanging plants to give it more warmth. The lighting was unflattering. The layout was strange. A professional decorator could do wonders for this place. If the owner was short on cash, maybe she could have made part payment with free meals or worked out some other kind of trade with a decorator.

The restaurant's waiter was friendly but was dressed in jeans and a T-shirt. He didn't look the part. Wait people don't have to be dressed formally but they should be dressed so that you can tell that they're not customers or dishwashers. In between waiting on customers, he sat at one of the tables reading a newspaper and smoking a cigarette. He looked like a customer and not a well-dressed or alert one either.

First impressions are important for any business. Since a camera doesn't lie, we used to take Polaroid photos of the inside and outside of our business. By studying them carefully we got ideas about signage, product placement and color scheme. When we did our first trade show, we built our own booth but hired a designer to help us with layout and color. He was well worth the expense. He made our booth look more professional and stylish. Even though our booth had nothing to do with our competence as manufacturers, it was the only way people could get to know us so it had to be inviting. That's true for professional offices, too. It's going to be harder to convince anyone that you're a competent accountant if your waiting room has cheap metal folding chairs and budget prints from K-Mart on the wall. Competent accountants are successful and successful accountants have nice offices. Perception is reality. Decor should be pleasant and inviting, whether you're an accountant, a restaurant or any other business or practice that is visited by prospective customers.

Well, we're into the fifth paragraph of this review and I still haven't talked about the food. That's because it is probably the least important part of the dining experience at a restaurant. Everyone thinks they're a food critic but mostly they're restaurant critics. They judge the total experience — the decor, the ambiance, the service and the demeanor of the staff. Food is only part of the experience. Furthermore, food made with the finest ingredients prepared by the world's most competent chef won't taste very good if it sits out under warming lamps for a while. Food must be served promptly. As in most other businesses, prompt delivery is very important. Incidentally, the food in this particular Mexican restaurant was OK but I'll never go there again. There are too many other nearby restaurants, Mexican and otherwise, that provide food which is just as good. They also provide a much better overall dining experience.

I hope that you'll learn something from this restaurant review — even if you're not a restaurateur. Whether you have customers, patients or clients, you're being judged based on their total experience with your organization. Make sure that you present a consistent, inviting image to them. If not, they may never come back.

Selling

Selling is the function that induces a customer to purchase a specific product or service.

In Section III, we discussed marketing. We discovered, selected, designed, or modified a product or service to meet the needs of prospective customers. Now we've got to turn those prospects into buyers. That's what selling is all about and that's what we'll be discussing in this section.

You've got to get rid of the cake you just made before you do any more baking. There's no need for bakers unless you've got takers!

Fourteen Keys to Big-Time Sales Success

In most businesses, sales is the most troublesome area. Usually, the sales function suffers from neglect. Either the owner is afraid of or hates selling and avoids it, or only sells when business is so bad the owner has, literally, nothing else to do. The company stumbles along with no growth or very low growth. The revenues are erratic and therefore, so is the cash flow. The company drifts from one crisis to another. If business picks up, the owner is afraid to hire more help because business might slow down again. So the owner becomes overworked and tired and makes mistakes and complains all the time. Then business falls off because the owner is so busy, he or she has no time to do the things necessary to ensure future business and is so tired, he/she does a bad job of servicing current customers. After a brief sigh of relief and short period of euphoria about not being overworked, the owner becomes cash-poor and panicky again, complaining all of the time about the lack of sales. These owners become chronic whiners and complainers, driving away customers, suppliers and prospects.

If you do any selling yourself, you've probably called on these people. When you solicit their business, they'll tell you, "I'm soooo busy I don't even have time to talk. I'm buried with work. Call me in four months." If you're a good salesperson, you'll put them in your reminder file and recontact them. Then they'll tell you, "Oooooh. Business is terrible. I don't have any money to buy anything from you. I'm just spending all of my time trying to keep the business alive." As a good salesperson, you'll probably just give them your card, tell them to call you if they ever want to buy something, put their name in the "dead" file and move on to concentrate on prospects who have some real potential.

I used to called on retail glass shops throughout the state of Oregon. There are many in the Portland metropolitan area but as you travel along the sparsely-populated Oregon coast, they become few and far between. There were two glass shops in a small coastal tcwn of about 4,000 people near the California border. One was owned by Dave, who was always out hustling business. I didn't get to see Dave often but I could always reach him by phone, particularly if it was right around 8:00 A.M. Dave always said business was fine. I could tell it was indeed fine because Dave's order rate was steadily increasing. When I dropped by Dave's shop, I usually met with his front-counter person who relayed Dave's purchase requirements to me.

Phil had a glass shop near the south end of the same town. Phil was always telling me how terrible business was. Phil bought very little from me but was always available to see me when I dropped by — except between 11:30 A.M. and 1:30 P.M. That's when Phil took his noontime break. Phil worked alone in his shop so he bolted the front door and settled down in his La-Z-Boy recliner in the corner of his work area and watched the noontime soap operas on his portable TV. During that time, he was unavailable to me and to anyone else, including customers. During the rest of the afternoon, Phil watched TV unless someone came in. Then he'd turn it off and wait on them.

Needless to say, Phil went out of business, though he didn't list poor sales as the reason for his business failure. Owners will say their business is failing because expenses are too high. Upon examination, you'll find their expenses are in line with other, similar businesses. These people aren't blowing their money on expensive cars or gambling junkets. Their expenses are high only in relation to their sales, which are too low. The expenses are already pared to the bone. The solution to their problem is to sell more! Someone else may say that things are tight because they're having a cash flow problem. Classical cash flow problems are usually caused by excessive inventory accumulation or slow-paying customers. When you look at their financials, you find neither the inventory nor the accounts receivable figures are out of line. Their cash flow is bad because they're going broke from a lack of sales.

The title of this chapter is "14 Keys to Big-Time Sales Success" but maybe it should be "14 Things You Can Do to Keep From Turning Into Phil." You may not be a soap opera buff but you may have selling as a very low priority on your "To Do" list. If so, you're risking business failure the same way Phil did. Here's how to prevent that:

1. Have a Plan.

If you're a small printer and you want to increase your sales, you've got to make some sales calls. How many? You decide. Twelve sales calls per week sounds like a good number. That's over 600 new contacts per year. If you visit with each of them and follow up as needed, maybe you'll get one-third of them as customers. That means you'll get 200 new customers each year. If each of them buys, on average, $800 worth of printing from you, you'll get $160,000 worth of new business within a year. If that's an acceptable figure, put 12 sales calls per week in your plan and set aside time to get them done.

2. Dedicate Time to Selling.

If your goal is 12 sales calls per week, then you've got to find the time to make them. Let's say that you can make six in-person sales calls in a day and still get to the shop at opening time and closing time. That means you've got to devote two days per week to outside sales calls. You need to allow another four hours or so for telephoning people, qualifying them, and getting appointments set up. This means you've got to devote two-and-a-half days per week to sales. Pick two outside days — say, Tuesday and Thursday. You block out your appointment book on those days. Now pick some times — say, 8:30 A.M., 9:45 A.M., 11:15 A.M., 1:00 P.M., 2:15 P.M., and 3:30 P.M. These are your available appointment times. When you call for appointments, don't say, "When can I come out to visit you?" Instead, say, "How about Tuesday at 11:15 A.M.? Would that be OK for you?" Most people can accommodate your schedule, especially if you can give them choices and options.

Since you're going to be unavailable to run the business while you're out selling, you'll have to put someone in charge. Pick an employee who is knowledgeable and trustworthy. Delegate Tuesday's and Thursday's work to your designated employee.

By setting aside time to sell every week, you'll see lots of prospects — in this case, 600 per year. Even if you're not a polished salesperson, you're bound to get some new accounts.

3. Smile. Never Show Anger or Annoyance.

You've surely met people who always seem to be smiling. They may not be. It's simply the way their face looks when it's at rest. You've also met people who are very pleasant once you get to know them but their natural facial expression is a frown or a look of sadness. It's not their fault. It's their natural facial expression. Many people do not have a natural "happy face." Practice smiling. Try to keep a smile when you're meeting prospects or customers. They will think you're happy to see them.

It is very important to never show anger to a customer. Some of the people you'll deal with are difficult but if you telegraph your annoyance to them, you'll lose them as a customer. Some people like to argue. If you get into an argument with them, you'll probably win because people who spend their business days arguing with others usually aren't very smart. By winning, you'll lose. You'll win the argument and lose the customer.

While placing a telephone order for some newsletter clip art, the company kept me on hold listening to music for five minutes, When the customer service rep finally took my call, I was greeted by, "Hi! This is Jim. I bet you've been on hold for a while because we're having an unusually busy day. I'm sorry you had to wait. How can I be of service to you?" What a great way to handle a customer! Remember that Jim was probably pretty stressed out himself handling other customers who had been on hold for a while. He handled the situation with a smile and made an enthusiastic customer out of me.

Remember the advice of Robert Half: "None are homely who smile."

4. Be Supportive.

It's not good enough to just refrain from picking fights with your customers and prospects. You've got to do some positive things, too. Make positive suggestions to your prospects.

> "Your idea is a good one but, you know, if we just relocated this ground wire to here, it would make your design more efficient."

> "The tie you've picked for this suit is very nice but you might want to consider this one too. It really brings out the color of your suit."

You get the idea.

Last year, when purchasing a color TV, the salesperson treated me rather curtly after I told her what I wanted. She said "You don't want that. You want this and here's why ..." She gave me good reasons for buying another brand and I took her advice. But I was put off by her manner. There was an implication that I was too stupid to make a good choice. It is important to use diplomacy and tact to get more customers instead of trying to prove what an expert *you* are.

5. State Benefits, not Features.

As experts in our field, we tend to fall in love with our own expertise and talk in buzzwords or skip right over the basics. It's a mistake to assume customers know as much about our field as we do. Recently, a printer pitched my business. "You should try us. We've got a new Heidelberg and it can do two-up printing." So what?! What does this mean to me? Does this mean my prices will be lower? The printing will be clearer? The turnaround will be faster? This printer has told me about a feature of his business but he's failed to tell me how his Heidelberg is going to benefit me.

"This car has twin turbos. That means that the spool-up time is less." That's a feature of an engine in an automobile. It does nothing to convey benefits to the prospective buyer. Here are the benefits:

"This car has a twin-turbocharged engine. Turbochargers allow us to use a smaller engine, providing good fuel economy when you're cruising. Step down on the gas and the turbos kick in, giving you the power and acceleration you'd get from a much larger engine. We use two smaller turbos because they will respond faster than one big one. With this engine, you get the best of both worlds — the fuel economy of a little engine and the power-on-demand of a big engine."

Note that we've stated benefits here — fuel economy, faster acceleration, instant response. We're explaining features in a way that a lay person can understand. It's OK to be obvious in stating benefits.

Don't you wish the folks who sell computers used more benefit statements when selling? I'm always confused by the mega-RAM, CD-ROM, platform architecture, bits, and bytes stuff. I just want to know what all of these things are going to do to get that computer to make me more money in my business.

Make sure that you use benefit statements when you call on customers or prospects.

6. Ask for the Order.

When my partner and I owned our plastics business, we knew a sales-man named Walt, who called on us about every six weeks. Walt provid-ed us with lots of information on industry activities and about what our competitors were doing, so we were always glad to see him. Walt would ramble on for an hour or so and would look at his watch and say, "Gotta go." Then he'd leave. Walt never asked us for an order. He never asked us how he could get more business. He never asked us how his compa-ny ranked compared to competitors. He never asked us if we bought from his competitors. We gave Walt about 10 percent of our total busi-ness. We gave the rest to two other companies. Their reps asked for orders. They'd ask, "What do we need to do to get more business? How can we do a better job for you?" We'd tell them, establishing a dialogue. They'd respond, giving us reasons and incentives to buy. We'd be favor-ably impressed and give them orders.

When you're out making sales calls, don't forget to ask for orders. "Can we do some business today?" "What's preventing you from giving me an order today?" "When do you expect to order again?" "If you feel that you'll be re-ordering in April, may I call you March 15th to see if you're ready yet?" When making sales calls, get closure. Don't leave an appointment with the customer telling you that *maybe* they'll give you an order *sometime*. You need to know whether or not they're going to buy from you, what conditions will influence their decision and when you can expect a decision.

Some of you are probably imagining a salesperson going out and phys-ically calling on customers at their place of business. Sales calls don't have to be in-person or outside. Sales calls can be made by telephone, in your office or shop, showroom, or retail store. Yes, retail store. Most sales people in retail stores aren't very good at selling. When a prospect walks in, sales clerks tend to ask questions which can be answered only with yes or no. Not — "Can I help you?" or "Are you looking for something special today?" Instead they should ask open-ended questions like: "How may I help you? or "How may I be of assistance?" By creating a dialogue, the salesperson can begin to get commitments. "What is stopping you from buying this suit today?" or "Oh, may I call you in two weeks when we get a new shipment of char-coal chalkstripe suits and hold one in your size for you?" Ask for the order. Get commitments.

If you're making a call and you don't ask for the order, you're not making a sales call.

7. Do Items 3 through 6 on a Regular and Consistent Basis.

Charles is one of my clients. His manufacturing company has been stalled at $550,000 per year in sales for the past four years. Profits are stagnant, too. Charles wants to grow. In this small company, Charles is the salesman in addition to being president, collections manager, chief designer, and scrubber of toilets. If you own your own small business, these multiple duties will probably sound painfully familiar.

Charles had been making one sales call every two months. Together we decided he needed to make five calls per week. I worked with Charles to help him set up a sales call program to fit his schedule. Wednesday was sales call day; Thursday was appointment and sales follow-up day. In six months, Charles' monthly sales had risen 14 percent. He was pleased. Then I didn't see him or hear from him for about a year.

One day Charles came in to see me, rather depressed. Sales were back down and Charles was sure the program had run out of steam. When asked how many sales calls he had made this month, his answer was, "None." The past three months? "Only three." The program hadn't run out of steam. Charles had.

You've got to keep making sales calls. You can't just smile and be supportive for a week and then revert back to your usual nasty disposition. You can't make a concerted effort to talk about benefits for a month or so and go back to using those incomprehensible buzzwords. You have to keep asking for commitments and orders, too. These are all part of your sales effort and that effort has to continue if you want your business to grow and prosper.

The answer for Charles is to grow the business doing the selling himself until he can afford to hire a full-time salesperson. In Charles' industry, he'll need about $800,000 in gross revenues to support a salesperson. He's getting there; in about eight months or so, he'll be able to afford to hire someone to do sales work for him. Charles wants to do this because he doesn't like to sell. Nevertheless, selling has been a valuable experience for him because, when he hires that salesperson, Charles will be wearing another hat — sales manager. It's important for him to under-stand selling so he can establish realistic performance goals for his new hire and monitor and evaluate the effectiveness of the new salesperson.

Keys 1 and 2 showed you how to lay out a roadmap for selling and a timetable for traveling down the road of sales. Key 7 says start traveling and keep doing it.

8. Be Timely.

When you make an appointment, arrive on time. If you get unavoidably delayed, call the customer or prospect and let them know what's hap-pening. Do you really expect people to believe your spiel about fast delivery and commitment to service when you show up 20 minutes late? The same goes for faxes, and phone calls. Return them promptly. If you're traveling, pick up your messages every day and return your calls. If you get someone's voice mail when you call back, leave a message and let them know when you'll be available to receive calls or tell them when you're going to call back.

If you have a store or office, make sure your doors are open and you're ready to do business at opening time.

9. Dress Appropriately.

Working for a Fortune 500 company, I dealt with salespeople from other businesses who called on me. Most of them were from other Fortune 500 companies. They dressed in a professional manner. Their clothes were stylish but subdued. Their accessories — pens, jewelry, briefcases, hand-bags, and the like were expensive-looking but not flashy. Later, in my own small business, I got to see how the rest of the world's salespeople dressed. Shocking! Salespeople were wearing T-shirts, leather jackets, jeans, Caterpillar caps, even old leisure suits! Many were poor salespeo-ple as well. Interestingly, the good salespeople who called on me still dressed well. The men may have traded in their suits for a sports jacket, but they still wore shirts and ties and had nice briefcases. The women may have traded in their tailored suits for a jacket and skirt combo, but they still radiated professionalism.

For many business owners and managers, others won't get to see your facility, your office, warehouse, or plant. They can only judge your firm by the way you present yourself. Clothing is a big part of that impression. In Chapter 44, two books about clothing are listed, *Dress For Success* and *The Woman's Dress For Success Book*. Both are written by John T. Molloy, who has made a career out of teaching people how to dress properly. Dressing properly does not mean dressing expensively. Tasteful and appropriate business attire is often less expensive than the garish and tasteless clothing for sale in the same store.

First impressions are lasting impressions.

10. Listen to the Customer.

Good salespeople love to talk. The best salespeople love to listen. Ask your prospect or customer open-ended questions so you can listen to what they are thinking. Learn what is motivating them. What are they buying? What benefit are they seeking? Low price? Product longevity? Safety? Instant service? Trusted advice? Improved profitability? You can't sell them until you know; you won't know unless you listen.

One of my clients, Bill, is a roofing contractor. He gets phone calls from prospects asking him to come out and look at their roofs and give them an estimate. Bill's company is not a cheap, fly-by-night outfit. He's been in business for over 30 years and his reputation is his salvation. Bill asks prospects numerous questions before he visits them personally. If someone needs to get a roof fixed because they're fixing the place up to sell it, Bill declines to visit with them. Those prospects have no interest in quality or longevity. They only want a low price. If the roof starts leaking in three years, they don't care. They won't own the house by then. If Bill finds a prospect who has a home that has been in the same family for generations, he'll go visit because they're a good prospect; or a business owner who values quality and has valuable merchandise in the showroom under that roof; or a church — where the decision is made by a building committee. None of the committee members wants to be held accountable if the roof doesn't last. Bill has learned to sell by asking questions. It permits him to qualify prospects. He doesn't waste time with those who are unlikely to buy, so he can devote more time to those who probably will buy from him.

11. Be Honest.

Many people are afraid that if they can't answer every question about the product or service they're selling, they'll be perceived as dummies.

Therefore, when asked a question about something they don't know, they fake it. They lie, hoping that the prospect won't realize it. This is a very bad idea. Most purchasing agents, middle managers and business owners have a very good "baloney detector." They know when a salesperson is faking it. It's much better to simply say, "I don't know but I'll find out." People don't expect you to know everything. They won't think less of you if you have to look something up, check with your supplier, or touch base with your office before supplying them with the information they need. They'll respect you for your honesty.

While going to college, I took a job at a TV and appliance shop. Eventually I became a salesperson for the shop, though my training consisted of reading some literature and being sent down the street to a competitor in order to hear their sales pitch. The salesperson was very good and gave me the full pitch complete with karate-chopping the plastic door liner on a new refrigerator to show how durable it was. It bounced right back, making a big impression on me!

Armed with this product knowledge, I took on my first prospect. I hammered the door liner, just like the other salesperson. Unfortunately it was a different brand of refrigerator and different plastic. With a loud crack, the liner split in two! A little knowledge is a dangerous thing. By trying to fake it, I lost a prospective customer. I would have been better off if I had said, "I'm not an expert in refrigerators but if you'll tell me what you're looking for in terms of size, features, and price range, I'll show you a few models which fit your general needs. Then we can get out the factory books and compare features and you can decide."

Don't try to sell unless you're prepared to answer questions honestly. If you don't know — say so!

12. Know Your Competition — Their Strengths and Weaknesses.

Every fight manager will tell you that a boxer must know the strengths and weaknesses of an opponent. The same is true in your business world. You can't compete effectively unless you understand your competition. In our business, we had a competitor, Marty's Plastics. Marty was notorious for not following customer blueprints and specifications and having to remake the item — sometimes more than once. Marty quoted prices which were about 20 percent lower than ours. When somebody asked for a quote, we'd always say, "Of course our price includes making it right the first time." For many of Marty's customers that was more important than price anyway and those were exactly the customers we wanted.

In our business, we also sold clear plastic sheet to glaziers and glass shops. Our competitor was a large multi-branch distributor. They had an outstanding reputation for service and delivery. The owner of the company, Hal, was a very personable guy who believed in calling on all customers even though they were regularly visited by Hal's sales force just to say thanks for their business. Hal never shied away from taking on the less pleasant tasks of selling, including notifying customers of price increases. Hal's company was prosperous, he dressed well, and drove a big yellow Lincoln Continental. I visited many of the smaller glass houses after Hal was there, driving right up to their door in my beat-up VW Scirocco wearing my off-the-rack sport coat. I'd point out that I was just another struggling small business owner like them. I'd ask, "Do you want to help Hal keep the gas tank filled in that big Lincoln or help me survive?" I'd mention that Hal's price increases were helping him save to buy another bigger, flashier car. The small glass shops empathized with me and gave me their business. My market share increased, my business grew, and within four years I was driving a new car — a Lincoln Continental. When calling on my smaller customers, I made sure to park down the street out of sight!

13. Don't Make Promises You Can't Keep.

"I'll call you back in five minutes." "I'll let you know when your car is ready." "I'll ship it today." How often has someone used these phrases on you and failed to deliver on their promise? If they don't call you back in five minutes or even the same day, can you really believe them when they tell you that they have the best on-time delivery of anyone in their field? If your mechanic fails to call you when the car is ready, you have a right to be skeptical when he says, "Of course I checked the brakes — I even road tested your car." If someone fails to ship that package today, can you honestly feel good about ordering from them again?

Think before you open your mouth. Don't say anything unless you can really do it. In my business, we made a habit of fibbing a little about ship dates. If we thought we could ship it by Tuesday, we told our customers that we'd ship their order by Wednesday. That way, if Murphy's Law kicked in, we'd still be able to keep our promise.

14. Before You Leave, Review Your Call and the Actions to be Taken by All Parties.

Whether you are selling at a prospect's office, over the telephone, in your showroom, or in your store, you must conclude your call by reviewing the actions promised by all parties before you take your leave. "*I'll* confirm product availability and let you know. You should be hearing from me in the next few days. *You* fax that credit application to our office by Wednesday so we can set you up with an open account by Friday." This technique will remind everyone about who's going to do what, eliminate confusion, and prevent misunderstandings.

Use these 14 keys and your sales troubles will disappear.

Techniques Change;
Basic Principles Don't!

Early in my business career, I was an engineer in a technical support group. We were often called on to travel to customer's locations in order to solve problems. One rule in the company was that engineers had to be accompanied by a technical sales rep. The salesperson was there to translate the blunt recommendations of engineers into words suitable for the customer.

Traveling with salespeople was a great learning experience for me. One of the best salespeople was Frank Moore, who willingly shared his secrets with me. One of Frank's secrets was to wear good shoes, so you had happy feet. This was a carry over from the '40s when salespeople did a lot of walking. If your feet were sore, you'd have a tough time staying upbeat on those sales calls. Frank suggested having a couple of pairs of shoes and, when you weren't wearing them, slip a shoe tree inside each one so they kept their shape. These days good shoes are less important to success. You drive to your client, park in front of their door and, at the end of the day, drive to dinner and your hotel. Tired feet are no longer a problem.

I did take Frank's other advice and it has served me well because it is timeless. Another thing Frank told me was, "Never make a call unless you have something to say." That's easy when you're meeting a prospect for the first time. It's harder when you're making follow-up calls. Frank would tear articles out of business magazines and hand them out to customers saying, "I read this and thought of you. I felt you might be able to use this information in your business." Great idea. In the '90s, we don't make in-person calls as much as people did in the '60s but there's no reason that you couldn't fax a copy of an article to a customer or prospect with a handwritten note. Let them know you're thinking about them and interested in their business.

Frank used to have some of his standard technical recommendations printed up to hand out to customers and prospects as he deemed appropriate. "People remember you better if you have handouts." That's still true today. Give prospects a concrete reason to remember you. Frank also kept detailed notes on his customers; he knew about their companies and about their families, too. "Did you buy that new scale for the shipping department you were telling me about last month? How's it working?" "Well, how's your daughter, Suzie, doing? Is she still at WSU?" Frank told me that you don't sell to companies, you sell to people, and the better you get to know them the better chance you have of keeping them as customers or clients — sound advice that's as relevant today as it was 30 years ago. Most sales contact software has plenty of memory available for storage of personal information about customers and prospects.

Technology changes specific techniques. You don't need shoe trees anymore. You don't need to carry change for the pay phone to call your office because you can now call from your cellular phone. I still use a Rolodex rotary card file because I like having those little paper cards right in front of me. But that's old-fashioned; you can get the same effect by installing a sales-tracking or contact management database in your laptop computer. All the software is useless unless you have basic techniques in place for gathering information in the first place, and much of that information may come from your present customers. You'll probably get it the same way Frank did — by asking questions.

Techniques may change, but the basic business principles are the same as they were in the '40s. To steal a line from *Casablanca*, a movie from the same era, "... the fundamental things apply as time goes by."

A Trade Show in a Box

"If Only I Had More Money, Everything Would Be Swell." Please feel free to sing along to this sad song, the National Anthem of small business in America. Well, guess what?! You won't get any money by singing the blues. The money's not going to fall out of the sky today or anytime soon, so you'd better learn to get along without it.

Part of the art of small business is getting things done cheaply and creatively. It's a necessary art since small businesses are always strapped for cash. When my business was small and cash-poor, we did a lot of dumb things but we did one thing which really worked well for us. It was inexpensive, creative, and it brought us lots more money. We called it our Trade Show in a Box.

We manufactured a line of products and were trying to set up a network of distributors. We'd telephone prospects and follow up with literature and more phone calls. Some of the people we contacted bought from us right away. Others demurred saying, "Why don't you come see us or maybe we can visit at the next trade show and see your products and chat." Well, we couldn't go see them; we had just enough gas money to travel 50 miles or so, but not enough cash for a cross-country jaunt on an airplane. We certainly didn't have the tens of thousands of dollars required to exhibit at a major national trade show. Yet we knew we somehow needed to get our prospects' attention and have an opportunity to strut our stuff. If we didn't, we'd probably never get them to buy from us.

Here's what we did. We ordered a bunch of white cardboard boxes. On each face we screenprinted a cartoon drawing of two characters dressed in tuxedos standing in front of a trade show booth with their arms extended in welcome. A cartoon banner said "Welcome To Our Booth" and had our company name underneath. We printed all this in bright red so it would be noticed. Inside the box we placed samples of our products and a letter which began: "Hi! Welcome to our trade show booth in a box. We would have had our exhibit at a regular trade show but we couldn't be sure you'd be there. So, we're bringing the trade show to you. If you'll please step inside the box, we'll show you around. Please watch your step there on the cardboard flap. To your left, you'll see one of our most popular items......" Well, you get the idea.

When that box arrived on our prospect's desk along with the day's mail, you can be sure we were the people who had the prospect's attention. Because our Trade Show in a Box was unique and people were amused by it, we got our follow-up phone calls returned. We also got orders. In fact, about 50 percent of the prospects who got The Box ordered from us within 30 days. A few sent us orders before we had the chance to do our follow-up phone calls with them. This program was amazingly effective. The program cost less than $60 per prospect, including product samples, packaging, and shipping. If we were having a good week, we'd send out 10 boxes. If we were strapped for cash, we'd only send out a couple of boxes.

In a two-year period, we picked up over $700,000 worth of brand new business with this technique. That was a quantum leap for our small company. Those new distributors kept on buying more and more from us each year, becoming loyal customers. Trade Show in a Box was the most successful program we ever did, whether we measured its success by percent sales growth, return on promotional investment, or real-live dollars.

How about a clever sales idea you can use to build your business? How can you get the attention of your prospects? Maybe it's some variation on the Trade Show in a Box idea. Or maybe it *is* the Trade Show in a Box! It's OK, please feel free to "borrow" my idea. Perhaps it will bring you more money and then you'll stop singing that awful anthem. Try it; it worked for me!

"I Buy Only on Price"

Regardless of what business you're in, someone is going to slam you about your prices. If you're a retail store, you'll hear, "Well, I can get it for less down the street." Wholesalers and manufacturers are always exposed to people who say, "I buy based on price." Contractors and service businesses often hear, "Your quote was a little high." There's always a hesitation on how to handle pricing objections. Allow me to offer you some suggestions:

Be sure price is a real issue here. Ask questions. "When did you see it at that price?" "What is the nature of your bidding process?" Sometimes prospects bring up price immediately as a defensive measure — they don't want to be thought of as suckers. Are they willing to modify their stand to something like, "I buy on the basis of price if all else is equal"? If so, that throws the ball back in your court to show that your product or service is superior and, therefore, commands a higher price.

One contractor who, when confronted with the I-only-buy-on-price issue, simply takes his business card and writes three names and phone numbers on the back. He presents his card to the prospect and says, "Let me save you some time. Here are the names and phone numbers of my three lowest-priced business competitors. Get bids from all of them and buy from the cheapest. Please hang onto my card though, because when the job is all screwed up you'll need to call me to get it done right. I cost more but I'm worth it." This is a pretty aggressive strategy and one that may be offensive to some but this particular contractor swears it works for him.

Ask, "Who have you bought from before and what has been your experience?" Many times this will bring out some horror stories about service or quality and will move the conversation away from the price issue.

For very competitive, commodity-type businesses, consider this. There's probably no more commodity-type business than the copy business. There are copy shops all over town and every stationery store with a copy machine is a competitor. Yet in many cities, copies are sold for prices ranging from $.02 to $.10 each. That's a 4 to 1 spread! What determines the price differences? Differences in location, convenience, and service. Many of you (and me, too) have purchased $.10 copies knowing they were sold elsewhere for 75 percent less. So much for all of us being "price buyers" at heart!

In my former company, we bid lots of jobs. In the early years we typically got 33 percent of what we bid. One day business was very slow, so we started making phone calls asking about old bids in order to figure out how much to cut our prices. The information we got was astounding. Of the jobs we lost, only 10 percent were due to price considerations and the average bid was 50 percent under our bid! If we cut our prices by that much, we'd go bankrupt! Of the other 90 percent — jobs lost due to issues other than price, we found that I could only address those other, service-related issues if we raised our prices. So at the end of the day, we did change our prices — raising them and using the extra money to improve service. Business got better and the shop got busy. My batting average on quotations went way up, too. We began getting 60 to 70 percent of jobs quoted. I started paying less attention to price and more attention to what was really important to my customers. You should, too!

Forget the 80/20 Rule, It's the 20/20/60 Rule that's Important!

Everybody who's been in business for more than, say, 10 minutes or so has had the 80/20 rule drummed into their head. Eighty percent of the sales come from 20 percent of the customers. Eighty percent of the problems come from 20 percent of the employees. Eighty percent of your shipments utilize 20 percent of your inventory. And so on. Some of the 80/20 rules are factual; others are baloney. It depends on the particular kind of business you're in. One rule that seems to hold true for every kind of business is the 20/20/60 rule. It's an important rule and it's not very well known.

Twenty percent of your prospects will love you and will immediately become your customers. It doesn't seem to make much difference what kind of business you have or what size it is. This rule is as true for restaurants as it is for machine shops. It's applicable to retail stores and professional practices, too. You've seen this rule in action. Somewhere you have a competitor who is dumb, obnoxious, and technologically obsolete. Yet some of his customers stick with him anyway and won't switch over to you. Loyalty is what you've been calling it. Love is a better word for it. These customers love your competitor and won't switch until your competitor goes out of business. You, too, have some customers who love you. No matter how far down your company slips and slides, they'll stick with you. Companies operating in bankruptcy still have loyal customers.

Twenty percent of your prospects will hate you and never buy from you unless you're the only supplier left on earth. They may not even buy from you then — they may choose to live without your product or service. There is no rational explanation for this, except for the well-worn phrase, "You can't please everybody." You may also refer to this as bad chemistry between your people and their people. In any case, there are prospects out there who hate you, or maybe they just love somebody else.

The remaining 60 percent of your prospects are those who are interested, but skeptical. They think that you might have something useful to sell to them but they need convincing. These are your most important prospective customers or clients, yet they are the ones we usually choose to ignore.

As businesses, we seem to spend all of our time and energy appealing to the two extreme categories. Perhaps we're designing new literature for our business. We always seem to create it to please the people, like Fred, who already loves us. Fred *will* love it and will probably give you lots of compliments about your new literature. So what. Fred already loves you and buys everything he can from you anyway. Treat Fred with respect and give him the good service he deserves as a loyal customer, but don't make him the target of your sales efforts. You should be designing your literature to reach out to the 60 percent of your prospects who are interested but skeptical. Your literature should answer their objections, resolve their doubts, and turn them into buyers.

Maybe you put all your energy into writing a great ad or sales letter thinking, "When Irma sees this, she'll change her mind." She won't. Irma hates you and nothing you say or do is going to change this. Stop designing ads for people who hate you; you're wasting your time. Irma will never consider you as her supplier. Instead, put your efforts into reaching out to those interested skeptics — give them a reason to buy your products or services instead of your competitor's.

Why do we all seem to fall into the trap of targeting the wrong people in our efforts? Part of the reason is we are urged to do so by lots of business books. Almost every book which has anything to do with selling or customer service has stories about sales turnabouts. These stories always talk about the Herculean efforts of a single salesperson to win over the account who repeatedly showed him or her the door. Such stories always have a happy ending with the reluctant prospect finally becoming a loyal and satisfied customer. These stories have great appeal to us because we all love unlikely stories with happy endings. We are all optimists at heart.

We love stories about climbing a symbolic Mount Everest but in real life most of us will not succeed as mountain climbers. In your business it's a better deal if you stay near sea level and play the odds instead of hoping for miracles. That's why you'll want to concentrate your efforts on those 60 percent — odds are they can be turned into customers.

Since we all love stories about success against formidable odds, here's one of mine. In 1982, I called on a small company that bought from my competitor. Their purchasing manager took an instant dislike to me. During our visit he remarked, "We'll never buy from you as long as I'm alive." Figuring that there was nothing to lose, I said, "Well then, do you mind if I telephone once a year to see if you've died?" He got angry and threw me out. I called every year and asked for him by name, reminding him I was just calling to see if he was dead yet or was at least feeling poorly. It got to be a standing joke with us and he started to warm up to me. In 1987, he finally started to order from me.

This makes a wonderful story but it's a terrible example of how to sell. The reality was this guy never really became a large customer, still gave a lot of his business to my competitor and didn't pay his bills very quickly. I would have done much better investing my time and energy elsewhere. In my business career, I've probably wasted too much of my time on hopeless causes. I would have been better off if I had simply concentrated on those prospects who could be reasonably motivated to buy.

So learn from my mistakes. Concentrate your business efforts winning over the folks who can be won over — that magical 60 percent of your market that has a genuine interest in doing business with you but needs a little persuasion. The other 40 percent will take care of themselves.

CHAPTER

27

If You Don't Have Good Salespeople, You Probably Won't Sell Much

Do you know what a 1957 Nash looks like? If you don't, hurry on down to your local public library and look in the Automotive History section. You'll probably find several photographs of it. Its styling is bulbous, disconnected, and trite. Regardless of the angle of the picture or position of the car, it looks bad. And most of the photos I've seen are flattering; the '57 Nash is one of those cars that takes a great picture — compared to the real thing. Who would buy a car that looked so ugly? I'm convinced that most of the buyers were salespeople. Salespeople can sometimes be the worst buyers in the world. They are suckers for a good sales pitch. Nash's slogan for 1957 appealed to the salesperson who drove from town to town — "Join the Swing to the Travel King — the New Nash For '57!"

If you've gotten far enough along in your business that you need to hire a salesperson, you're probably replacing part of yourself. Most business owners do the selling themselves when the company is small. If you've grown the business to the point where you need someone else to sell, you've done a pretty good job of selling. That means you are a salesperson yourself and you're a potential victim for any prospective candidate with a good pitch and a polished trial close. The purpose of this chapter is to give you some guidelines for evaluating and hiring candidates for that sales job of yours. Regardless of the kind of business you're in or the kind of product or service you're selling, a good salesperson must have four basic traits. They are:

1. Hungry and Motivated.

Salespeople won't perform well unless they want to and unless you provide incentives to help motivate them. You must carefully scrutinize all prospective hires to make sure that they're hungry enough to sell. One of my clients, Frank, hired a salesman named Jack to sell casualty insurance. Jack had great credentials but was a lazy fellow who never put forth much selling effort. He worked short weeks, took long lunches, and was always on the phone with his friends. Jack's life had recently changed. His wife had gotten a big promotion with a correspondingly big increase in salary. Jack had recently settled a lawsuit from an old accident that had left him with a permanent limp; the settlement was substantial. Finally, Jack had recently inherited some money from his dad's estate. Jack was living in his comfort zone. He didn't need extra money and was no longer the hotshot salesman of a few years back. Frank finally fired Jack. Jack landed another sales job at another agency. He'll probably hop from agency to agency until he runs out of employers or until he decides to retire. He is living off of his past reputation.

There are lots of Jacks out there. Make sure you don't hire one. Look for a salesperson who needs the money. Some of the best salespeople are those who live a little beyond their means. They'll be very receptive to bonuses and incentives. In my company, my lead salesman made bonuses which accounted for almost 50 percent of his base salary. He sold hard because he needed that bonus money to make those house and car payments. Whenever I saw him drive up in a new car, I smiled. I knew that we were in for some big sales increases in the near future!

2. Good Work Habits.

Any salesperson you hire must be there to help your business, not hurt it. Sales personnel must be able to keep reasonable records — customer information, quotations, expense records. Every good salesperson is organized. The sloppy and disorganized ones are mediocre at selling. During the interview process, ask the prospective sales hire how they keep records at their present job. If they travel, how do they set up travel files when on the road? Their answers or lack of answers will be most revealing.

3. Smart.

"He's such a dummy, we'll move him into sales." I overheard this remark in my very first job. I couldn't believe the mind set of the individual who said it. Unfortunately, there is still part of our culture that believes salespeople are just a bunch of jovial, friendly fools who blunder around the marketplace in search of orders. Nothing could be further from the truth. Good salespeople are very intelligent. They are also quick thinkers. In the world of selling, you must be quick on your feet. I can take a fairly unintelligent person and make them a good production worker. It's easy to instruct someone in running a machine, packing boxes with merchandise, filling out forms, or flipping burgers. Every sales call is a little different and a salesperson must be quick-witted enough to shift mental gears between customers.

Our company had a production worker named Ned. He was a personable young man so we moved him into sales. We didn't give the whole matter a lot of thought. We trained him and sent him on his way. He was a disaster. Ned was incredibly stupid — he lacked common sense. Customers complained about him. He forgot orders. The final straw was when Ned flew to Los Angeles for a meeting with a major client. His rental car broke down on the freeway. Instead of abandoning it and calling a cab, Ned spent 45 minutes under the hood repairing it. Ned showed up a half hour late and filthy dirty for this meeting with a Fortune 500 company. The company thought we were hayseeds and never gave us any business. I offered Ned his old production job back at his old wages, but he refused and quit. The only good thing to come out of it was he went to work as a salesman for a competitor!

4. Honest.

Salespeople represent you to the outside world. If they represent you in a less than honest way, your reputation will suffer — not theirs. If you hire a dishonest employee for your shop or office, they'll steal from you. If you hire a dishonest salesperson, they'll steal from you and your customers.

Any salesperson you hire must be used to and experienced with your kind of selling. Otherwise you need to plan on spending time and dollars "untraining" them from their old sales habits and training them in the sales habits required in your business. Your kind of selling breaks into two general categories — degree of relationship and mode of selling.

Degree of Relationship

This term defines the depth of involvement that needs to be established and maintained with the prospect/customer. If you sell moving services to homeowners, you don't need much of a relationship. It's your job to get the order and move on. It's unlikely that the customer will buy from you again. If they do, it will be years away. You want to give them a good moving experience but you can't afford to spend a lot of time hand-holding. You need to close the sale during your visit with them or in a one-shot telephone follow-up. If you don't, it's unlikely that you'll get the order.

Contrast this with selling an automotive component to General Motors in Detroit. If you're trying to sell a new "miracle" kind of wheel bearing to this industry, you've got a long road ahead of you. The sales cycle from initial contact to purchase order may be three to four years. There will be preliminary discussions with the new product evaluation team, coordination with test engineers, discussions with the R&D group, contacts with chassis and performance engineers, meetings with platform/product managers, and negotiations with the purchasing department as well as hearings before the vendor assessment group. As a salesperson, you've got to find and support "champions" for your idea at every level in GM. You must develop fairly close relationships with many people along the way. This is heavy relationship selling. It is common when selling major products or services to major corporations, institutions or the federal government. If you're not selling a major component product, the process is simpler — it's a lot easier to sell pencils to GM, for instance.

Most small businesses don't have heavy relationship selling but they do have some need to establish a relationship and continued dialogue. If you're selling property and casualty insurance to mid-sized businesses, you'd better establish rapport and involvement with your buyer because the policy needs to be reviewed regularly and renewed annually. In my own manufacturing business, we needed to establish and maintain relationships with our customers who purchased items on a weekly or monthly basis. Hiring someone who had sold one-shot things like moving services wouldn't be a very good idea. We'd have to retrain him or her to deal with relationship selling.

Small businesses like video producers, point-of-purchase display producers and T-shirt and banner screenprinters need salespeople who can
qualify or close quickly on the first or second call. Their customers are a
diverse bunch who buy only occasionally — maybe once every two to
five years. They would probably not be well served by a salesperson
who traveled around and sold caulk to glaziers. That person is used to
calling on a specific group of customers and builds sales by frequent
contact (by phone and/or in person) and by establishing a relationship
with the prospect. The caulk peddler would be confused by the different
pace, outlook, and expectations of the banner maker.

Sometimes there's no personal relationship. If you're selling by direct
mail or on the Internet, you need pleasant order-takers rather than people who do outbound selling.

Modes of Selling

Next you need to consider your Mode of Selling. There are two basic
modes with sub-categories within each mode.

Business-to-Business: Your customers and prospects are other businesses. Businesses buy for rational reasons and will typically take a
value-added approach to buying. Your salespeople usually need in-
depth product knowledge. They will be expected to be experts, able to
make specific recommendations to the prospect. If they sell primarily by
phone, they better have a pleasant voice! Try to conduct part of your
new sales hire interviews with your back turned so you can evaluate an
applicant's vocal personality. In my business, all of my sales staff did
some telephone selling. If they sell primarily in person, their overall
demeanor had better say "business professional." That includes voice,
physical appearance, grooming, dress, and behavior.

Speaking of demeanor, my friend and printing supplier, George the
Printer (whom you'll meet again in Chapter 30), once hired a new salesman named Lucifer. My office overlooked the parking lot and when I
heard this tremendous rumble outside, I thought we were being invad-
ed by the Hell's Angels motorcycle gang. I looked out and saw this beat-
up, 10-year-old Mercury sedan with a rotted vinyl roof pulling in. It
obviously had no mufflers. My phone rang and I turned back to take the
call. About two minutes later this apparition appeared in my office,
wearing a red-burgundy suit with a maroon sport shirt which was open
halfway to his navel. It was Lucifer. He was wearing a gold chain

around his neck with a crooked gold horn attached and had a greasy black mustache and equally greasy hair which was combed down over his forehead. He had pushed past our receptionist, bullied his way down to my office and said, "Hey, get off the phone. I want to talk about youse buying more printing from us." I threw him out. George finally got rid of Lucifer but only after he had cost poor George three customers.

Business-to-Consumer. Your customers and prospects are consumers. You're selling pest control services to homeowners in person, you're selling carpet cleaning services by phone, or you've got a retail store and your salespeople are there to deal with walk-ins. Consumers buy for more emotional reasons and will frequently buy because they like the salesperson. Your salespeople need less product knowledge and more ability to ferret out what motivates the prospect. Consumer telemarketers are trained to go for the numbers — make lots of calls, use a short standard pitch, and get an order/appointment then quickly move on. Rejection is very high but, if you make 200 calls in an evening, you'll get a few appointments or orders. This is a lot different than business-to-business phone selling. Consumer telemarketers will have to be retrained if you're going to have them sell to businesses.

All of these things are important if you're hiring an outsider to be your salesperson. What about hiring from within your own company? In my manufacturing business, that's where most of my salespeople came from. My point-of-purchase and department store sales manager came from my production plant. Rusty had been one of my plant foremen. He had demonstrated good work habits and had good people skills. I sent him to a three-day sales workshop and then made joint calls with him for a few days. Rusty became an excellent salesperson and his technical knowledge was impeccable because of his experience in our plant. Many of his customers wanted custom-made items and Rusty knew what was buildable and what was not. He could often make suggestions to improve the manufacturability of a product and, thus, reduce the price — saving the customer money. The customers respected Rusty and listened to him. They saw him as a valuable resource. Rusty was clever enough to use his manufacturing skills to build customer relationships. In your business, it may pay to look inside your firm before you go outside.

Selling by Outsiders

It is impossible to finish a discussion of selling and salespeople without discussing independent reps and distributors. Many small business owners mistakenly believe they can eliminate the hassle of a salesperson by using reps or distributors. Let's look at each.

Reps are independent agents who will represent you in selling your product or service to prospective customers. They are paid nothing until they make a sale. Once a sale is made, they are paid a commission by you to compensate them for their sales efforts. Commissions range from three to four percent for high-volume commodity items to 10 to 15 percent for specialty items. Reps pay their own travel, entertainment, office and telephone expenses. Many reps are highly successful, making incomes well above six figures. Most reps derive the majority of their income from a single company's product or service line. Successful reps are not normally inclined to handle the product or services of a very small business. Their success depends on keeping their customers happy. They know intuitively and by experience that small companies cause problems — irregular and unpredictable product supply, inability to provide support before and after the sale, lack of professionalism from the owner. If there are problems, they will reflect badly on the rep and may adversely affect sales and revenue from his or her principal product or service. Successful reps usually have a full platter anyway and are not inclined to add new products or services from unknown companies to their plate. Even if they take on your line, they will probably not showcase it — they have more important things to sell and feature at each call. If their customer shows a lot of interest, they'll respond and provide more details. Otherwise your line will be stuffed into the bottom of their briefcase never to be shown at that account again. Reps have to worry about putting food on their own table each night and will focus on the things which bring the most revenue to them.

If all of this sounds like a condemnation of independent agents — it's not. It's just that most small business owners have unreasonable expectation of reps. Small business owners think of using independent reps as a way to avoid selling. It's not. Every business who uses reps successfully has an in-house sales manager to supervise the care and feeding of their rep force. If you've got an independent insurance agent, go buy him or her a cup of coffee and ask about the support provided by the home office. You'll be surprised how much help they are given: leads, practice enhancement seminars, training of the rep's new employees and salespeople, and much more. A good rep organization can be a wonderful selling machine but only if *you're* prepared to make a big commitment in time, people, and dollars to support it.

Distributors are used for products rather than services. Distributors buy directly from you, take title to your product and often take physical possession of the product, too. They make their money by buying it from you at a discount and reselling it to a customer at full price. Distributors get discounts of 30 to 50 percent depending on the product and the market. With a distributor organization, you'll still need your own salespeople who will sell to and service your distributors. The benefit of distributors is that you need far fewer salespeople than if you sold the product directly. Distributors work best with standard products that are easily understood. If every product you sell is a new invention or creation, you'd better not use distributors. They don't do well at selling abstract ideas. Distributors will do a great job selling your Model TK-2000 handtruck. They will not do well selling your "tell me what kind of products you're trying to move around in your warehouse and we'll invent a novel device that may somewhat resemble a handtruck but will be a lot better" line.

In my plastic manufacturing business, we sold a line of 500 stock display products, things like clear plastic signholders, shoe displayers, and the like. We had a catalog in which every product was illustrated and was assigned a part number. A separate price sheet was available — distributors got discounts of 40 percent off those posted prices. We had over 180 distributors nationwide. We had a sales manager who handled all sales matters with our distributors including setting up new ones and finding out what kinds of other products were needed for our next catalog. He was supported by two order-takers, one of whom functioned as a customer service representative to handle distributor problems. It was a successful arrangement. Please note that our use of distributors did not save us from having sales personnel.

The use of reps or distributors will not magically take away your responsibility for selling your product or service. You'll still need a salesperson in-house to coordinate your sales efforts. Remember, a good salesperson is probably the most important single person in your business. Hire carefully — hire correctly.

Customer Service

The sour taste of poor service lingers long after the sweetness of low price is gone. Think about a product or service you purchased six months ago. Do you remember the item? The packaging? The color of the tablecloth at the restaurant? The cleanliness of the showroom or office? Probably not. Do you remember how you were treated? I bet you do. Customer Service describes the behavior and standards that are expected by customers and prospective purchasers. In this section, we'll discuss how to prosper by taking good care of the most important people in your business — your customers.

It doesn't make any difference how long you slaved in the kitchen to make that cake, or how good it tastes. If you offend people when you serve it, they won't be back to ask for seconds.

Customer Service
Ain't What It Used to Be!

We've got a real problem in this country and the name of that problem is Bad Customer Service. Every year, highly-paid professional seminar leaders fly all around the country giving more and more talks about improving customer service. Every year seminar attendance grows; business people are spending more money than ever trying to learn how to provide better service to their customers. Every year the *actual* level of service experienced by *actual* customers seems to get worse and worse.

Consider this. Forty years ago, there were no seminars about customer service. Forty years ago, when you pulled into a gas station (they used to be called service stations), uniformed men with bow ties would appear around your car to fill your gas tank, clean your windshield, check your oil, put air in your tires, happily make change and thank you and ask you to come back again.

Today, you get your own hands dirty while pumping your own gas and checking your oil yourself. Half the time there are no towels or water for you to clean your own windshield. If you need to put air in your tires, it costs a quarter. No one asks you to please come back again.

Forty years ago, telephone operators at businesses personally greeted you and directed your call to the proper party. Today, you'll get voice mail and a complex, time-consuming decision tree. When you've made a decision and pressed the right buttons, you'll as often as not get disconnected.

Forty years ago, car dealers made car buying fun. Every year, before the new models came out, dealers moved new cars into the showroom in the dark of night and whitewashed all the showroom windows so you couldn't see in. People got curious and excited. Prospective buyers and former customers were invited to preview parties hosted by the dealership. The service bays were scrubbed spotless and were full of shiny new automobiles. People got caught up in the excitement and bought cars. The cars in the showroom looked great with glittering chrome and whitewall tires. (All the cheap cars with no chrome and blackwalls were parked out back near the dumpster.) When you took delivery of your new car, you were introduced to the service manager who presented you with his card and gave you a personal tour of the parts and service departments.

Today, you probably won't be attending any parties. The new models look just like last year's. All of the cars in the showroom today have no chrome and wear blackwall tires, but they're not cheap! You're lucky to get anybody to even talk to you at many car dealerships unless you're ready to buy *right-this-here-minute*. After you buy a car, you may get to meet surly and ignorant service writers who know nothing — except how to add up bills.

Forty years ago, department stores were theaters of wondrous things. They seemed to have every piece of merchandise ever made and took a real pleasure in showing off their goods. Displays and store windows were imaginative and inspiring. Clerks were attentive and knowledgeable. Today, it's still theater but it's a one-act tragedy — indifferent clerks, merchandise which is poorly displayed and zero service. Specialty stores like the Gap, Williams Sonoma, The Limited, The Museum Store and others have taken over the retail business because the department stores let them.

Well, as terrible as this all may be, this can be quite an advantage to you in your business. The level of customer service forty years ago was so high that you would have had a real hard time standing out from the pack. Your customer service would have needed to be incredibly exceptional — out-of-this-world, in fact. Today, it's easier. If you'll simply give *ordinary* customer service, you'll be perceived as *exceptional*. Here are the five secrets of ordinary customer service:

1. Do What You Say You're Gonna Do.

If you promise your client preliminary sketches by Tuesday, make sure you meet your commitment. If a client or customer changes the scope of work in the middle of the project, don't assume that the client knows these modifications will change the completion date. Advise clients of any such changes immediately so they can deal with their impact. Otherwise the client may think you're failing to keep your promise. If you agree to produce 500 parts for a job, be prepared to produce a small overrun so that you don't come up short. If your store opens at 10:00 A.M., be sure to have your doors open and be ready to handle customer transactions by that time. If your voice mail message says, "Your call is really important to us. Please leave your number and we'll call back." Call back. Don't say it unless you mean it.

2. Be Consistent.

At our house, the trash company picks up on Friday mornings between 11:00 A.M. and 1:00 P.M. About 50 percent of the time, it's between 12:15 and 12:30. The recycling people pick up on the same day, sometime between 6:00 A.M. and 6:00 P.M. and it's different every week. We have to get our stuff out early in case they show up early. Sometimes the recycle bins sit out in the pouring rain all day waiting to be picked up. The perception is that the trash company is a "better" company than the recycle company, even though both are fulfilling their contractual obligations to the community. How about your company? Are you perceived as inconsistent and, therefore, unreliable?

3. Underpromise and Overdeliver.

If you repair and resole shoes, surprise your customer by giving the shoes a quick polish. A local commercial real estate developer does a fine job but adds a special touch by presenting his clients with a framed watercolor of their new building. The cost is minuscule compared with the cost of the overall project and it builds client goodwill. In an earlier chapter, delivery dates were discussed. Remember, if you think you can do it by Tuesday, tell your customers that you'll have it by Wednesday. That way, if Murphy's Law kicks in and you don't make that Tuesday date, your customers won't be disappointed or angry. And if it's ready on Tuesday and you call them and tell them so, they'll be pleasantly surprised. Offer your customers pleasant surprises rather than unpleasant ones.

4. Extend the Same Courtesies to Others You'd Expect Yourself.

Never forget basic civilities. Simple phrases like "Please hold" make a far better impression than "Hang on a minute, will ya?" When disconnecting, don't place the handset back in the cradle. To the party on the other end, it sounds like you're slamming the phone down on them. Just press the disconnect button with your finger. A click sounds better than a crash. Don't forget the basic courtesies of "Please" and "Thank you." Make sure your employees use them too.

Please consider using these basic techniques of courtesy to help improve your image and build your business. *Thank you* for listening.

5. Do It Promptly or Not at All.

When I called to place an ad in a business publication, their voice mail urged me to leave a message, extolling how important my call was to them. A message was left but the publication never called back. A week later, another call was placed; we received the same voice mail message. Three months later we finally got a call back, with no apology for being so late in returning the call. Needless to say, we were no longer interested in placing an ad with them.

If you'll re-read all five of these customer service secrets, you'll find they all have something in common — they don't cost anything. They're absolutely free! There is no state or federal law saying you have to pay employees extra to say "Please" or "Thank You". It costs you no more money to hang up the phone quietly. Being consistent may actually save you money! Promptness is a zero-budget, zero-expense item.

We may never again experience the thrill and drama of a new car introduction party, but old-fashioned service from car dealers or anyone else is an attainable goal. Voice mail is here to stay but with good equipment and intelligent usage, it can be made into an asset which helps bring you more business. If a department store's service is slipping, it doesn't mean that the service level in your business needs to slip along with it.

Stand above the pack. Reinstate good customer service in your organization. Make your customers feel welcome and they'll come back to buy again.

Do You Have
Gatekeepers? Or Thugs?

Back in the really old days, salespeople or drummers made appointments by telegram, took the train to town, and were welcomed by the local tradespeople. They were a novel diversion during an otherwise dull day on the prairie. They dispensed interesting and vital information and only showed up when the train came to town. Later, there were more of them. They showed up unannounced in their own cars, appeared at more frequent intervals, and were less welcomed.

When the gasoline crisis occurred in 1973, salespeople started using the telephone to conduct business. This was novel and it worked well. Then, the phone company offered courses called Phone Power about how to sell by phone. More people started selling over the telephone and they were less welcomed.

Then the phone companies were deregulated, long-distance rates plummeted and business people were deluged with phone calls from salespeople. Con artists got in the game, too, selling everything from phony oil leases to fake Dali art prints over the phone. People got fed up and appointed someone inside their businesses to screen their calls. These screeners have become known as gatekeepers. It's their job to find out why someone is calling and direct their calls to the appropriate party. Most are pleasant and professional; some are thugs.

Here are some horror stories collected from friends, clients, and my personal experiences. They are all true. The names and circumstances have been changed to protect the guilty.

One of my clients called to get a job quoted. "Send a letter and a sketch," he was told by a gatekeeper. He did. When he hadn't heard anything in a week, he called again. After an exhaustive screening ("They asked me everything but my shoe size"), he was told, "We probably threw out your letter. We get hundreds of pieces of junk mail." He took his several thousand dollar job to their competitor who was glad to get the business.

I met someone at a business function. "Please call me next week," he said, referring to a specific matter which he brought up. He wasn't a prospect and I had nothing to sell him. He was asking me for a favor. I called the following week. "Mr. Jamsley won't be talking to you." "But *he* asked me to call *him*." "He doesn't talk to salesmen." "Well, that's fine but I'm not a salesman and he asked me to call him." "You don't understand. Mr. Jamsley doesn't talk to anyone." Mr. Jamsley can get his favors elsewhere.

When contacting a law firm, one of my friends was asked, "What is this call in reference to?" She explained she wanted to set up a meeting with this particular attorney who had been recommended to her. She was asked to provide more details. In four sentences she explained the specific nature of the matter and also gave the source of the recommendation who was one of the lawyer's larger clients. "I'm sorry that's not specific enough. You'll have to give me more before I'll put you through." My friend hung up and gave over $12,000 of legal business to another, more receptive firm. She goes out of her way to badmouth the first firm to anyone in town who will listen.

There are more horror stories but you've gotten my point. Before you say, "That's not our company; we don't do that," you should try calling your own place of business from an outside phone and see what happens. You may get an unpleasant surprise.

The Only Business
You "Own" is Your Own

My good friend George the Printer did high quality work at very good prices. George helped me out in a lot of ways and, over the years, has given me many valuable suggestions about how to get the most for my printing dollar. George the Printer ran his business in a chaotic and, sometimes, unreliable way. The work usually came out right but deliveries were almost always late. When George told us that he'd have a job finished in a week, we'd plan on two weeks and usually be right. Sometimes, when we ordered 1,000 pieces, George shipped 1,200. Other times we got 983. But George the Printer was a good soul and did fine work, so we overlooked his shortcomings.

When my business sold, I introduced George to the general manager appointed by the new owners. I took him aside and told him the new management would not be as forgiving about his shortcomings as we had been and recommended that he put his best foot forward with the new owners. George nodded earnestly and said he would. Six months later, I needed some personal printing work done and called George. As usual, his quote was good, his work was crisp and clean, and he delivered it to me one week later than he said he would. We had a nice chat and I asked him how he was doing with my former company. "Those @#**! dumped me." said George. "After all the good work I did for the last eight years, too. Ya know, Joe, there's no loyalty anymore at that place since you left. I put in eight years taking care of that company and I deserved to keep that business. I worked hard; I did good work ... well, gosh, I figured I 'owned' the business at that account!"

Sorry, George, that's not the case. Nobody "owns" the business but the owner. If you've got a restaurant you may lose your most loyal customer after only one bad dining experience. Your customers have the right to a good experience *every* time. If you fail to meet their expectations, they have a right to feel shortchanged and take their business elsewhere. If they find what they need elsewhere they may never come back to you. You don't "own" the customer or their business.

Isn't it funny that we spend lots of effort as well as promotional and advertising dollars chasing and wooing new prospects while we pay less attention to our existing customers and clients? Isn't it strange that we'll fawn and fuss over the special needs of a new customer while we consider the requests of an existing customer to be an imposition? "They want what?!! Who do they think I am, Santa Claus?!!" Isn't it odd that when someone has taken the trouble to come personally to our store, office or plant, we'll make them wait while we talk to an unannounced, unqualified prospect who calls on the phone?

Remember the lesson of George the Printer. Don't take any of your customers for granted — even if they've been buying from you for years. Don't assume that because they have already bought from you before they'll tolerate something less than your best efforts. You don't *own* them. You don't own their business. The only thing you *possess* is the money they've paid you for their most recent transaction. The only thing you *deserve* is their goodwill from their last transaction. Customer goodwill is something you never *own* — you *rent* it on a transaction by transaction basis. If you disappoint the customer, your rental agreement is canceled. That means you have to start over finding a new customer who'll extend you some goodwill and some future business. Of course, you won't "own" that customer's business either. The only business you ever "own" is your own.

Lemon

The April, 1994 issue of *CAR*, a British automobile magazine, didn't have the usual car photograph on the cover. Instead, there was a full color photo of a yellow lemon with a VW insignia on it. Inside was a devastating report on the Volkswagen Golf. After an extensive 40,000 mile long-term test, the testers at *CAR* mused that it was a good thing that everything else in life isn't as unreliable as the Volkswagen they tested. Wow! What a public relations nightmare. How would you like to be the president of Volkswagen AG? How would you like to have that kind of negative publicity for your company?

Well, this chapter isn't about Volkswagens, cars, or even about public relations. It's about quality. You see, quality problems were what made *CAR* call the VW Golf a lemon. Quality is not just for manufacturers; it's for every type of business. Quality is not an absolute term; it's based on customer expectations. Nobody expects an apple to stay good for a year; we do expect the tires on our cars to last that long. No one will be surprised to see a plastic lawn chair fall apart after 15 years but a house better not. The quality of brain surgery is not determined just by the skill of the surgeon but also by the post-operative care, the management of pain, and the effectiveness of physical therapy afterward, as well as the bedside manner of everyone involved.

Quality means giving the customer, client, or patient a positive experience as well as a successful outcome, based on customer expectations. Recently, I made some purchases in a local bookstore. The selection was easy; the store ambiance was adequate, and the price was right. But the transaction was marred because the clerk was in training, didn't know how to work the register or process credit cards and had to be guided step-by-step by a supervisor. It was maddening. When the bill was presented to me, I said, "Where's my training discount? After all, if I have to stand here for five minutes and role-play being a customer while you two practice being employees, shouldn't I get a special discount just like employees get?" Well, I didn't get my discount and I won't be back either because that store has got a quality problem. The outcome was successful in that I got the book I wanted but the experience wasn't positive because of staff quality problems.

Statistics show that happy customers tell five of their friends about their good experience. Unhappy customers tell 11 of their friends about their bad experience. Only 1 in 25 dissatisfied customers complain directly to the owner or manager of the business. Instead, those 25 unhappy customers relate their bad experiences to 275 of their friends! Over 90 percent of unhappy customers will never purchase from you again. So forget about winning back lost customers. Spend your efforts improving your quality of product and service so they don't leave you in the first place, and bad-mouth you to all their friends.

Any business can have quality problems, including service businesses. CPAs who don't return phone calls. Attorneys who make you wait for 20 minutes when you've made an appointment and show up on time. Landscapers who show up hours late. Even something as simple as forgetting to activate your voice mail or turn on your answering machine so your phone rings and rings when you aren't there reflects on you and your business. It gives the customer a negative experience rather than a positive one.

How's your quality? Are you giving customers and customer wanna-be's a positive experience and a successful outcome? Are you meeting their reasonable expectations? If not, it's time to make changes now.

Employees

If people like those cakes you bake, they'll soon be asking for more. That's great, of course, but you'll soon be needing some help. You'll need to get reliable helpers who share the same cake-baking values that you do. People who are willing to work using your recipes — not theirs.

In this section, we'll help you to find workers who will follow instructions, be nice to your customers, and won't spit in your batter!

How to Hire (and Keep) Great Employees

Most of us have a poor track record for hiring. Many business owners tell me they have to hire three to six employees to get one that's a "keeper." That's because of the way we hire. We look for people who *interview* well rather than people who *work* well. Or we fail to define and communicate what we actually want our employees to do.

Recently, Barry, the owner of a trade show exhibit company, claimed that he hasn't been able to grow his business over the last three years because he couldn't get and keep good help. Barry employs six people. His turnover is so bad that last year he sent out 62 W-2 forms. That represents an annual personnel turnover of almost 1,000 percent! He claims that this is an exhibit industry problem. Baloney! In the same three-year period, two large exhibit companies in the same town had grown over 50 percent, creating and filling over 40 new jobs. Barry's little exhibit company is stalled because Barry doesn't do a good job of hiring people and has never defined his requirements and expectations of his new hires.

A. The Hiring Process

There are five steps you must take to hire a great employee:

Contact is the first step. How do you find new employees? Most people start with an ad in the Help Wanted section of the local paper. If you decide to run an ad, you must be specific about what the job is. State the hours of work. Set forth the experience level you require. Make known any special skills required. If the job is for a delivery driver, state that a valid driver's license is required. Being specific in your ad will eliminate applicants who don't meet your requirements. That means less applications for you to wade through.

My quest for employees started with asking others for recommendations. Begin by asking your good employees if they can suggest someone. Some great employees have been gotten this way. If employees have bozo friends (and we all have some of those), they won't put them on their recommend list. They know their advice will reflect on them. They'll stick to suggesting good people. Fellow business owners and people in the community are also good referral sources. Over 60 percent of new hires come from initiative (they call and ask if you've got an opening), networking, and recommendations.

The same source reported that 10 to 15 percent of all hires come from placement agencies. Theoretically, they do some of the pre-screening for you. But, remember, there are lots of placement agencies out there, so ask for recommendations from fellow business owners in your community. Choose an agency with a good track record.

Talk with fellow business owners. It's a good idea to become active in your business community. Join the chamber of commerce or some other local business group. It's helpful and useful to keep in touch with fellow business owners.

Application is the second step. You need to have a standardized application for prospective hires to fill out. You can get these from any office supply house. Don't use an old application; as laws about hiring practices change and evolve, these forms change, too. One old one from the '50s asked applicants to state their race and religion. This is illegal! Don't try to save money by using applications from your grandfather's old Studebaker dealership!

Ask applicants to come in and pick up an application, take it home, fill it in, and send it back. Their willingness to do so shows their degree of interest and initiative. If they have a résumé, they're welcome to staple it to the completed application but insist the application itself be filled out.

Take the stack of completed applications and review them. Look for neatness and completeness. If the prospective employee has unintelligible handwriting, how can you expect this person to work in your business?

If the application is dirty, smudged, and crumpled up, it speaks volumes about this prospective hire's work habits. If there are unexplained holes in the employment history section, be suspicious. Don't call them in for an interview. Typically, interview 25 percent of applicants. The other 75 percent either have inadequate qualifications or haven't made a good first impression.

The third step is the **Interview**. Bring every prospective employee in for an in-person interview. Meet them face-to-face and look them in the eye. It is better to spend plane fare and reject a candidate instead of hiring a bad apple who sounds good on the phone. If possible, set up your interviews for the same week — even the same day. That makes it easier to compare one applicant with another.

During the interview, ask the normal questions about job history. But, let's face it, there are some people whose real talent in life is interviewing. They do great interviews and make lousy employees. You've probably already hired a few of them. They are Professional Interviewers.

Use a couple of questions to try and sort things out. First, ask, "Where do you want to be in five years?" There's no right answer to this. Simply try to find out if the applicant has any goals in life. People who have no goals tend to drift from job to job because they don't know what they want. You'll do everything you can to keep them happy. Then they'll read an article about life in Costa Rica and suddenly announce they're quitting to move there. The goals question is a good one but it's commonly asked. The Professional Interviewers will handle it with grace and aplomb with a well-rehearsed response. That's why I have another question.

The one I ask came from Bob Brehm, who was my plant superintendent. He used it to see how quickly people think on their feet. The question is, "What's the best thing that's ever happened to you since high school?" Now, of course, there's no right answer to this. Most people will stall and stammer a little before they answer this unexpected query. If you've got an applicant who's been sailing through the interview like a Hobie Cat on a calm lake in a light breeze and suddenly there's dead silence coupled with a look not unlike a deer caught in your headlights ... POW ... you've just bagged a Professional Interviewer. The question is unusual enough they don't have a prerecorded answer. Suddenly, they have to think on their feet.

Here are some other questions you might ask: "What's the smartest thing you've done in your working life so far?" "What's the dumbest thing you've done in your working life so far?" "How do you plan your day?" "What was the best job you've ever had?" "What was the worst job you've ever had?"

What we're trying to do here is to flesh out the applicant from the rough pencil sketch in the application and résumé.

If you expect this person to spend much time on the phone, turn away from them during the interview and listen to their voice. Does it inspire confidence? Does it have a nervous timbre? Is it screechy and annoying? I once hired a woman who made a great impression in person. She had a great smile, had good eye contact, and was expressive with her hands. As a disembodied phone voice she sounded strident and whiny. She was a wonderful employee but we kept her away from the phone.

Typically, you'll probably interview three to four candidates to find one great employee.

The fourth step is **References**. You must call three personal references and three previous employers before you offer anyone a job. Do your reference checking right after you finish your interview with the candidate. It is amazing how few owners actually do this. They hate to do it because it takes time out of their busy day, but you must make these calls. You'll find them most enlightening. Here are some responses volunteered by various references. They were talking about people I was ready to offer jobs to:

- "after he got out of jail"

- "except for that lawsuit she filed against our company"

- "when he's sober"

- "except for her chronic shoplifting problems"

- "her ex-husband came to the plant and threatened to kill her supervisor"

So, be sure to check all references. If you have more than 30 employees, you can have your plant manager or general manager do it. Otherwise, don't delegate it. Do it yourself. When you contact references, be sure to ask open-ended questions:

- What was his/her biggest accomplishment?
- What was his/her biggest challenge?
- Is this person eligible for rehire?

If you're calling a large company's human resources department for a reference, you'll probably get the standard big company line, "It's our policy to only confirm the dates of employment." If your prospective employee was a stellar performer at his or her last job and has any smarts, he/she will have given you the name and extension of a former supervisor who will provide candid and deserved praise. Expect to get stonewalled by the human resources department but if the candidate's direct supervisor gives you corporate gobbledygook, start worrying.

Now, it's time for step five, the **Offer**. Be prepared to make an offer within two days after you interview the candidate. An offer is a legal thing, so be sure to state your offer clearly and precisely. If there are moving expenses allowed, lay out the conditions and limits. Outline your employee benefits. If the offer is complex, confirm it in writing by letter, fax, or e-mail, so there are no misunderstandings. Don't hesitate to pay a little more for a great employee; they're worth it.

Put on your sales hat and sell the offer. Ask for a commitment. Have them start within two weeks, so they don't have time to shop for a better deal.

Now that you've got a great new employee on board, you've got to work to keep him/her!

B. Keeping Great Employees

Keeping deadwood employees is easy. They'll stay no matter how you treat them. Keeping great employees is hard work. You must keep them interested, motivated, and rewarded. You've got to have a system for doing this or you'll risk losing them. There are six steps to keeping great employees:

The first step is **Having Rules**. Early in my career, I worked for a boss named Hassad who was famous for coming by my office at quitting time and asking inane questions about my daily work accomplishments. These sessions would drag on and on and I would typically leave work 30 to 45 minutes after quitting time. I therefore felt justified about having a casual attitude about showing up on time. One morning as I sauntered into work 20 minutes late, Hassad's boss, Gus, called me into his office and showed me a chart he had been keeping about my arrival times. I protested, saying that I was putting in more than my fair share of time each day. Gus would hear none of it. "I don't care when you leave, no one is asking you to stay late. We expect you to be here on time and put in a full day's work." This was my first lesson in rules. At that company, showing up on time was a big deal and, as an employee, I was expected to abide by their rules. I was never late again. That evening, when Hassad wandered in at quitting time and began his vacuous interrogation about the status of my various projects, I said, "Let's discuss it in detail. How about tomorrow morning at 8:30? Are you free then?" Of course, Hassad wanted to discuss it now. I told him that my work day was over and that I had outside commitments to keep. After a few days of this, Hassad left me alone and went on to pester someone else at quitting time. This would have never been a problem if someone had taken me aside on my first day and told me which rules were really important.

Your company has its own culture. As the business owner, you have initiated and encouraged this culture and are very particular about certain items. You need to clearly communicate your rules and expectations to your new hires. These should be in the form of an employee handbook. Chapter 36 will go into more details about rules, policies, and employee handbooks.

The second step is **Having Files**. You should create a file folder for each of your employees. The file folder should contain basic data on each employee including their original employment application. At our plastics company, we had little half sheet pads with the title "Employee Incident Report." We used this form to confirm verbal warnings, issue written warnings, and report when an employee had done something "above and beyond the call of duty." When it came time to review employees, we could use these slips of paper as a reference. All of the good and bad incidents were in one file location. All business owners tend to remember the bad things done by employees; an employee file is a way of helping you remember the good things, too.

The third step is **Performance Evaluation**. You need to create a system to review all employees at least every six months. Tell him or her what he or she is doing right; tell your employee what needs improvement. It's a good time to review wages as well. If he or she is doing a great job, let him/her know that, too, so your employee will be less inclined to begin floating résumés and job applications elsewhere.

The fourth step is **Terminate Bad Employees Quickly**. The cliché "A bad apple spoils the bunch" is especially appropriate here. A bad employee makes marginal employees think they can get away with the same thing as the bad apple. Good employees get frustrated and feel that their superior performance is unrecognized. Bad apples make you lose respect as a manager. Be decisive. Fire sub-par employees immediately.

The fifth step is **Fix Things That Make Employees Leave**. A local fish cannery laid off half of its work force. Many of their ex-employees applied for jobs with us. We hired several. In the initial employee reviews (we did them after 90 days on new hires), they all said it was a wonderful place to work. When asked why, they said, "Because we don't have to work in 40-degree refrigerated rooms and it doesn't stink of fish." Then summer came. Shop temperatures rose to the mid-90s. A few of the cannery people told me they were leaving. Upon conducting exit interviews, they said, "It's sooo hot out there. Are you too cheap to have fans or something?" We went out and bought several floor fans. Purchasing fans was far cheaper than hiring a bunch of new employees. Our other employees appreciated the gesture, too.

Reducing employee turnover can save you a lot of time and money. Find out why employees leave. If the reasons are something you can fix, do it.

The sixth step is **Create a Reward System**. This is so important that Chapter 34 is devoted to it. When I sold my business, almost every employee was on an incentive bonus program of some kind. The establishment of bonus systems raised average employee wages by 25 percent. Their productivity improved by over 80 percent, so the bonuses cost me literally less-than-nothing, and my turnover was cut by two-thirds. Bonus systems pay off if they're done properly.

In Colin Powell's autobiography, *My American Journey,* he speaks convincingly of the need for good subordinates and tells of listening to a talk given by Admiral Hyman G. Rickover, the father of the nuclear submarine. Rickover stated his philosophy that endeavors succeed or fail because of the people involved. Only by attracting the best people will you accomplish great deeds.

Every moronic big company has a slogan which says something like, "Our Company is Only as Good as Its People." The saying itself is absolutely true, but many big organizations are too bloated and mismanaged to identify, get, and keep the best. Their incompetence in dealing with their workers is why cartoonist Scott Adams sells so many "Dilbert" books. He's struck a true chord in the workplace. As a nimble small business, you have the ability to find, hire, and keep great employees. Now ... go get 'em!

CHAPTER

33

... And Then
Wendell Died and Almost
Killed the Business, Too!

When my partner and I bought our business in the 1970s, it came with one asset that wasn't listed on the company's books — Wendell. He was our plastic fabricator and prototype maker. Wendell was a wizard when it came to producing things. He could find the most efficient and easiest way to produce incredibly complicated shapes and designs. Wendell had a pleasant personality, too. That made it easy for us to turn customers over to him — "Just tell Wendell what you want and he'll make it for you." Wendell handled our customers' requirements, answered their questions, made the things they wanted, called them if he had a question about their project, and let them know when their order was ready. He took care of everything except sending out invoices and collecting the money.

Now you would think after making detailed models and prototypes all day, Wendell would go home and play some sport or just zone-out in front of the TV. He didn't. In his spare time, Wendell built model airplanes from complicated and intricate model kits. They cost hundreds of dollars and took hundreds of hours to complete. Wendell loved to do this stuff in his spare time. Amazing. He had an eye and a mind for detail.

Wendell had two shortcomings. First, he almost never wrote anything down. On those rare occasions when he did, it was unreadable to anyone but Wendell. He carried very complex specifications around in his head. Wendell could get away with this because he had an excellent memory and almost total recall. Wendell's second shortcoming was he was a hypochondriac. In any small plastic fabrication shop, workers would occasionally scratch, bruise, scrape, or cut their hands. Much of the work in progress had sharp edges and you might get a small cut just moving work around. That's not any different from working at a glass shop, an automotive body shop or a cabinet shop. We always kept bandages and disinfectant available to deal with small scrapes on the spot. Any time Wendell got a minor scratch, he would make a big scene. "Owwww! Owwww! Look at this. Ooooh! The skin's all raw. I hope I don't get blood poisoning from this! Or ... lockjaw!"

Because Wendell whined and complained about every little scratch, no one ever took him seriously. So when Wendell complained of chest pains one night, insisting that his wife drive him to the hospital and demanding the doctor admit him for observation, no one ever thought that Wendell might really be sick. Until he keeled over and died of a massive heart attack during visiting hours the next day. Wendell was 29 years old.

We felt badly about Wendell's death but we felt his loss even more keenly when customers came around to ask about the status of their projects. Only Wendell knew and he took his secrets with him to the grave. We had to start several projects over from scratch because no notes could be found and we couldn't figure out how to finish the half-built piece Wendell had created. Months, even years later, customers would call and say, "Have Wendell make us another part like he did last time." We'd have to ask them bring in the old part so we could measure it, make drawings, and try to figure out how Wendell built it. We swore we'd never get into a situation like this again. We began to generate detailed drawings for every new part we made. We put together a manufacturing plan for every project, and preserved it. We assigned job numbers for every part or project we did, created folders for each, and stored them in newly purchased file cabinets. We learned our lesson.

How about you? Do you have a Wendell in your business? Lots of small businesses do, you know. What will you do if your Wendell dies, or quits, or goes to work for your competitor? Can you replicate the work your Wendell has produced — whether it's a manufactured product, a customer profile list, a financial analysis report, or a bookkeeping system?

Insurance agents always like to talk about "key individual" insurance. And that's probably a good idea. The best insurance isn't just an insurance policy — it's a back-up system created by you so you've got access to the knowledge, the contacts, and the information your key employees carry around every day in their heads. If you don't have one, get started on your back-up system today..

A Bonus for All Seasons

My frustration with standard bonuses and incentive programs began while working for a large corporation. Performance bonuses were normally given out around the end of the year. "A bonus for the Christmas season," they said. If mine was smaller than I expected, the response was, "Well the company didn't make as much money as expected." Who cares! It wasn't my fault that the R&D Division blew a lot of money on some turkey of a product that didn't work. I excelled at *my* job and expected to be rewarded for it. Later, in my own company, we lost Mark, one of our best production workers when he said, "I'm twice as productive as any other employee you've got. Starting tomorrow I want a 100 percent raise or I quit." Doubling Mark's pay would have put him outside of our established wage ranges. We didn't give him what he wanted, so he left.

In our growing plastics manufacturing company, my partner and I were always looking to improve productivity. Over a two-year period, we tried a couple of incentive programs that didn't work. Our employees were excited at first but interest soon dropped off. One said, "This is like some kind of religion. It's full of mysteries and miracles. When we don't get a bonus, it's a mystery; when we get one it's a miracle." Others accused us of rigging the program to cheat them out of their money. We realized that the real problem was the employees didn't understand the program and didn't feel they could influence the results. They were frustrated and so were we. We decided to start over from scratch. We made four rules:

First, it was OK to have different programs for different groups of workers. The goals, output, and productivity of the shipping department are clearly different than those of salespeople, so a different reward/bonus system is necessary. Ultimately, we had five distinct bonus plans in place — each for a different group of employees.

Second, each program had to be understandable to employees. Calculations had to be as simple as possible. All data used to calculate bonuses had to be shared with employees. If they didn't get a bonus, they would know why. They would know what steps they needed to take to get extra pay in their next check.

Third, the bonus had to be based on things the individual employee or group could control. It's not the responsibility of the warehouse workers to make an overall company profit. It's their job to pack and ship goods in an efficient and conscientious manner. We paid them a bonus based on value of goods packed per employee-hour with adjustments for mistakes.

Fourth, all bonuses had to be paid quickly. If you only pay out bonus money at the end of every quarter, the employees won't remember the January mistakes that offset their stellar performance in March. They'll feel that they've been cheated out of their bonus. We paid bonuses either monthly or bi-weekly.

Our production workers were on a piecework-style bonus program. They were paid for each task. At the end of each pay period, we added up the piece rate payments for each worker. If the payment totals exceeded their wages based on their hourly rate, we paid them by piece-work. If it didn't, we paid them based on their base hourly rate. Since they were guaranteed a minimum base rate they wouldn't be penalized if they had a bad week. They still had a living wage so they could pay their bills. Our indirect workers, foremen, lead workers, etc., were on a bonus program based on the ratio dollar production output per indirect hour. If they could get a lot of product produced without a lot of super-vision hours, they made more money. If they exceeded our monthly tar-get by 10 percent, they were paid a 10 percent bonus on all wages for the month. The warehouse crew was also given a bonus based on dollar value of goods shipped per employee hour. If they exceeded their target by 14 percent, they got a 14 percent bonus except we made downward adjustments for excessive mistakes, miscounts, misshipments, and dam-age caused by poor packing. To get a bonus in the warehouse, you not only had to be fast, you had to be careful, too. We had two different bonus programs for our sales staff — one for direct sales; the other for sales through distributors. Both included a substantial base pay rate with bonuses for sales above a certain monthly target. Our targets had built-in seasonal adjustments so sales bonuses could still be earned even during our slow season. See Figure 34.1 for an example of a warehouse bonus program.

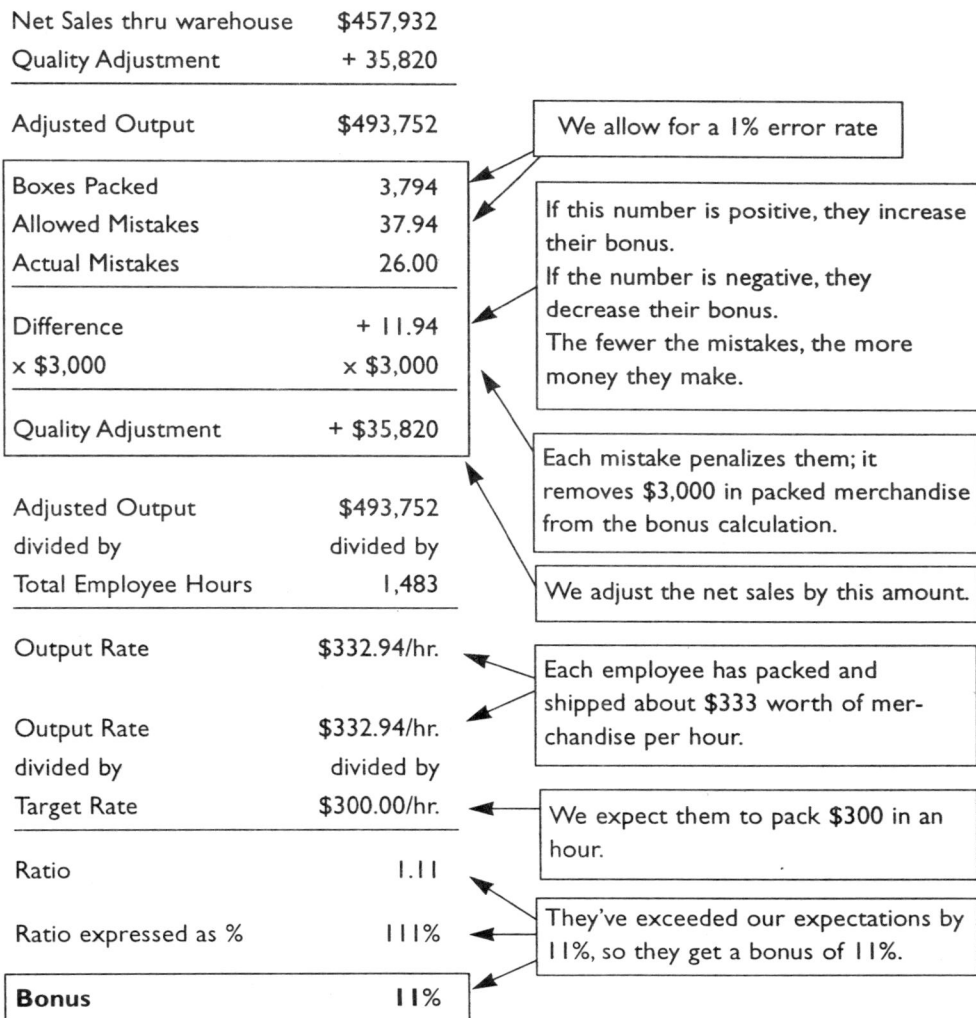

After we started implementing these programs, we found they produced several benefits. First, productivity soared. After six months, our

Figure 34.1: An Example of a Warehouse Bonus Program

Net Sales thru warehouse	$457,932	
Quality Adjustment	+ 35,820	
Adjusted Output	$493,752	We allow for a 1% error rate
Boxes Packed	3,794	
Allowed Mistakes	37.94	If this number is positive, they increase their bonus.
Actual Mistakes	26.00	If the number is negative, they decrease their bonus.
Difference	+ 11.94	The fewer the mistakes, the more money they make.
× $3,000	× $3,000	
Quality Adjustment	+ $35,820	Each mistake penalizes them; it removes $3,000 in packed merchandise from the bonus calculation.
Adjusted Output	$493,752	
divided by	divided by	
Total Employee Hours	1,483	We adjust the net sales by this amount.
Output Rate	$332.94/hr.	
Output Rate	$332.94/hr.	Each employee has packed and shipped about $333 worth of merchandise per hour.
divided by	divided by	
Target Rate	$300.00/hr.	We expect them to pack $300 in an hour.
Ratio	1.11	
Ratio expressed as %	111%	They've exceeded our expectations by 11%, so they get a bonus of 11%.
Bonus	**11%**	

production workers had increased their output per employee hour by over 80 percent. Second, employees came up with creative ideas to further improve their output. Assembly tables were rearranged. Several home-built "tools" to improve productivity were developed. One employee was quite tall and raised up his assembly table with cinder blocks. He found it made him more comfortable and boosted his output. One day he was very upset because he couldn't find the cinder blocks. He went out and bought his own and brought them to work every day. After work, he returned them to the trunk of his car and drove home. No one would ever "steal" his cinder blocks again!

Employees gave us real feedback — about equipment improvements, layout changes, and even product design. They came up with ideas and inventions because these things could put more money in their pockets. Our warehouse employees asked us for rubber stamps with each person's name. They would stamp their name on each outgoing carton. They wanted to know each employee's "batting average" so they could help the worst employees to improve by copying the best. We also found that overall employee turnover dropped in half. Employees were making a lot more money and felt in control of their destiny. They now perceived our company as a good place to work.

Don't think that incentive programs are problem-free. First, any incentive program won't work unless you have good historical data from which to draw. How long does it take to cut 300 plastic pieces? To stitch a three-inch facial laceration? To prepare a monthly P & L statement for a retail shop with 600 transactions per month? To put together a monthly newsletter for an insurance client? To design a new logo package for a start-up company? How many boxes can a warehouse employee pack in a day? What is the approximate dollar value of goods in each carton? How many deliveries can a driver make in a day? How have sales varied month by month over the years? Do these trends vary for the different markets which you serve? Several companies have jumped headfirst into an incentive program without having any idea what the baseline needed to be. They failed. You can't establish benchmarks without some history to back them up. Any bonus program initiated with insufficient historical data will be like a house built on a quicksand foundation. It is destined to sink.

Another problem was that the piecework segment of the bonus program created a great deal of information to manage. We had to add one clerical employee for every 12 or so production workers to keep track of the piecework bonus calculations. We even held "piecework court" when an employee claimed the rate for a particular task was too low. Even with these added burdens, we still had a more profitable company — the productivity increases more than offset the added costs.

An additional concern is you may be **paying** bonuses during a month when you're making little or no profit. **Remember,** you're rewarding employees for what *they* control — it's not their problem if you're less profitable because you've had to write off bad debts, priced your product or service too low, or went nuts and bought three new Jaguars for company cars. As the business owner, profits are *your* problem. If the customer service group earned a bonus because they did an exceptional job, you are obligated to pay them whether you've had a good month or not. Your obligation to them is as strong as your obligation to your bank loan. You don't try to weasel out of paying your loan installment by telling your banker you've had a bad month, do you? Don't do it with your employees, either. By the way, with a good bonus system in place, bad months will be a thing of the past. Your employees will be pulling together to make every month a good one.

You should recognize there are some people who will not be comfortable with incentive programs. We hired people who later quit because they didn't like the "pressure" of having their efforts measured. Thankfully, they were a very small minority.

Another potential problem area is quality. You must have good quality control programs in place before you start your bonus program. If you don't, employees will sacrifice product or service quality to get speed. You must establish minimum standards to be met.

Finally, there are some jobs that may not fit a bonus program. Our receptionists were not part of our bonus program. We couldn't figure out how to quantify their work. They had little control over the number, type, and duration of incoming calls per day. How do you measure the balance of pleasantness and efficiency required in a good phone receptionist? You can't have them rushing customers, prospects, and suppliers along just to get high phone contact numbers — that would be perceived as rude. We just tried to make these support people well paid, comfortable, and happy. We hoped they would pass their good feelings along to people who telephoned.

Speaking of the telephone, one day we received a call from Mark. He wasn't happy with his new employer and wanted to know if we would take him back. He had heard about our incentive program and wanted to be part of it. We gladly rehired him. Mark finally got paid what he was worth.

The Worst Employee in the Business May Be You!

Look, I realize that you work very hard in your own business. You're the one who has to pay the bills. You're the one who stays awake nights worrying about the business's survival. You're the last one paid (if there's any money left) after you make payroll. So, it's understandable that you sometimes feel a need to do crazy things, break all the rules or vent your anger at work. After all, you're the boss. Resist the temptation. Don't do it!

Employees are great mimics. They will emulate your attitudes, your work ethic, your emotions, and your outlook. They will telegraph these attitudes to your new hires, your suppliers, clients, patients, or customers. Grouchy doctors always seem to have grouchy nurses and receptionists. Ditzy store owners create and surround themselves with ditzy employees. What makes things even worse is that some owners like to hire people who are just like themselves instead of trying to find employees who bring strengths to areas where the owner is weak.

If you're giving bad habits to your employees, you're the worst employee in your business. How can you find out if you're in this category? There are seven warning signs I call the Seven No Ones:

1. No One Else Is More Dedicated.

This is the Boss-As-Martyr Syndrome. All business owners feel this way deep down inside especially after a bad day. The trick is to never telegraph this attitude to your employees. While some may give you some superficial sympathy, they will be offended by this attitude. Their mental response is, "Hey. Nobody asked you to own your own business. You're probably making millions doing this, so stop whining to me. I've got problems of my own." Boss-Martyrs try to make employees feel guilty and inadequate. Instead they get resentment. The other problem is the second half of this "No One" sentence is often, "therefore, I deserve … to buy myself a fancy new desk … to be a day late with payroll … to scream and curse at my workers or perform some other irrational act." You're the business owner. It's your money at stake. You shouldn't expect employees to be as dedicated as you. If you set the right example, you'll be surprised how dedicated your employees can be.

2. No One Else Can Do It.

Back in Chapter 32, I mentioned Barry and his little exhibit company. Barry honestly believes no one can build an exhibit piece better than he can. He also feels his customers deserve nothing less than a Barry-made exhibit. With this attitude, Barry will soon become a one-person company. His employees can't meet his impossible standards. Barry is so busy making stuff that he won't take the time to train his new hires properly and lay out his expectations. Instead he gets mad and curses them for their inadequacies. The employees (who are much-in-demand skilled carpenters and cabinet makers) quickly depart for a workplace where their efforts are appreciated. Business owners often hide behind the excuse, "I can do it faster than I can train someone." You'll find them running through the shop grabbing tools out of employee's hands or in the office snatching someone else's computer keyboard. They never learn to delegate and can't grow their businesses because they're too busy, as one owner once said, "rescuing my company from the paws of idiots." I know who the real "idiot" is here. Do you?

If you want your business to survive, you must learn to delegate. You must learn to recognize when you are overloaded and find a competent employee who can handle it.

3. No One Else Cares.

This is an attitude expressed whenever big things go wrong. We once had a large job that required taking cut pieces of acrylic and annealing them before assembly. We annealed acrylic by stacking the cut pieces in an oven and baking them overnight at 180 degrees Fahrenheit. Our oven had a dual-scale temperature gauge and one of our employees mistakenly set it for 180-degrees Centigrade, which is almost 360-degrees Fahrenheit. No supervisor on any of our three shifts ever checked the oven. The acrylic fused and the result was a very big $8,000 discolored plastic brick that was totally unusable. Was I angry? You bet! Did I care about losing $8,000? Heck, yes! Did my employees care? Of course, but not as much as I did. Did I fire anyone? No. What I did was to paint over the Centigrade scale so this mistake would never be repeated. The employees involved were properly contrite and learned to check their work more closely. I never telegraphed the "No One Cares" attitude. I would have gained nothing and would have wrecked our morale.

I related my giant acrylic brick story to a fellow owner who had just experienced a big employee screw-up in his own business. He replied, "That's fine for you but my employees are a pack of morons." Never being a master of the tactful phrase, I asked, "And what moron hired them?" It was he, of course, and he was not amused. His employees weren't morons, they were just imperfect human beings. This owner wanted to savor the pain of this mistake rather than learning from it and setting up systems to prevent its reoccurrence.

4. No One Else Deserves This.

When things go well, some owners want to take all the credit themselves. They forget to thank employees who made their success possible. They pocket the money and don't share the wealth. This is a great way to lose good employees. That's why I advocate incentive systems — ways of rewarding employees when they make good things happen in your business.

In our business, we established the Benjamin Award, the presentation of a crisp $100 bill (with Ben Franklin's picture on it) to any plant worker who gave us a good usable idea. It was presented publicly and inspired other employees to submit ideas, too.

5. No One Can Find Me.

An owner of a $2 million heating and air conditioning business spends most of his day hiding out. He hides from employees and angry customers. His business isn't working anymore. It's grown and he's now frightened of it, so he disappears. He has abdicated control and leadership. The business is losing money, too, and he can't pay his bills, so he hides from suppliers as well. I've seen this happen twice before. Both companies folded. If your business is frightening you, get help. If, after reflection and advice, you're still frightened, get rid of what's scaring you. If you feel your business is too big, downsize it or sell it. Don't abdicate.

6. No One Else Has Better Ideas.

In our small business, my partner and I hated to give money back to customers. If we invoiced it, we mentally considered it to be a done deal. If we had to write credit chits because of shipping damage or a customer wasn't satisfied, we, irrationally I admit, felt those customers were reaching into our pockets and stealing our money. I hated the tasks of haranguing with customers about merchandise credits. Even though I tried to put on a pleasant veneer, I was telegraphing my attitude right at the customer. Finally, Dave Kern, our distributor sales manager, came to me and asked to take over the program. He felt we were angering customers and that this was costing us business. He had some clever ideas about handling customer service and proposed a budget (tied to sales levels) to do refunds and credits. After some agonizing, hand-wringing, and second guessing, we let him run with it. He did a fine job — much better than I had been doing. The customers were happy. Dave was happy. We were happy because customer service became a predictable, regular expense. Thanks, Dave. You saved me from myself.

7. No One Else Is Better at Pulling the Stunts I Do.

Welcome to Management-by-Brinkmanship. There are owners who have bizarre codes-of-behavior. They try to cheat customers but get mad if their employees try it. They try to hustle departing employees out of their final paycheck, but don't understand why employees steal from them. They sexually harass their assistants and are shocked when employees harass fellow workers. They fail to realize they are leading by example. The phrase "Do as I say, not as I do" doesn't work in small business. Your employees will tend to be just like you. Be good and so will they.

Small business is not a democracy. Small business owners do not engage in Management-by-Popular-Vote. They are people with ideas, drive, and passion. They started their own businesses because they wanted control and power. That makes them tyrants. Good business owners are benign tyrants, getting employee input and being responsive to worker needs, while still controlling the business. Benign tyrants surround themselves with strong, helpful employees.

Bad tyrants rule with an iron fist. They are the worst "employee" the business can have because they crush the spirit of their real employees. Their businesses are unhappy little fiefdoms where the rule is "Do it my way or don't do it at all." They surround themselves with workers who are weak sycophants. Like all bad tyrants they are overthrown, in this case, by their competitors who run their businesses sensibly, encourage ideas, and run circles around the tyrant in the marketplace.

Who Rules Your Business?

Pardon me for stating the obvious, but most people you hire have worked somewhere else. They've picked up rules, procedures, and habits (good and bad) from prior employers. Take those various habits multiply by four or five employees and you've got a cacophony of noise instead of the sweet sound of an orchestra. To make an orchestra, you've got to create your own arrangements — your own rules.

Employees like to live an organized life. They like to have rules. If you do not establish any rules in your workplace, you won't suffer anarchy and chaos. Your employees will simply make their own unwritten rules. Their rules will strike a balance among what is good for them, what they are used to, what they are comfortable with, what they think they can get away with, and what they think is good for you. They won't tell you the new rules right off the bat, so you'll be confused and unhappy. When you finally figure them out, you won't be very happy with some of their rules. That's why you need to make your own rules, in writing, in the form of an employee handbook.

Al has no employee handbook. He owns a garage door service and repair company. He lets his installers take the company trucks home but insists they keep them clean and shiny. They don't. Al never orders them to do so. He just quietly seethes and occasionally grumbles to them, "The trucks don't look very clean." They laugh off his comments because they don't take him seriously.

Julie owns a trophy and engraving company. Her front counter people have no authority to grant open account status or credit to customers, but they do anyway. Last year Julie's bad debts exceeded her net profits. Julie has never disciplined an employee for violating one of her basic work rules because she's afraid they'll leave. That might be the best thing that's ever happened to her business. Her profits would probably double.

Ernest, who owns a $2 million printing company, has his sales people complete and mail out all invoices. They won't do them in a timely manner because they don't like paperwork and would rather go out and pitch customers. Invoices go out, on average, three months late! They're always undercharging the customers because, by then, they've forgotten what work they did for them. Ernest has cash flow problems. He can't get loans because banks take one look at the Receivables on his financial statement and laugh at him. Ernest has over $500,000 of uncollected old receivables on the street. When challenged about his sales staff's refusal to do paperwork in a timely manner, he defensively responds, "Yeah, but they're soooo good at selling."

Many business owners shy away from having rules in an employee handbook. They think it's too complicated to produce one. Not so. When we only had five employees, we issued our own handbook. It was easy. We simply took a handbook from a Fortune 500 company, and used it as a guide to create our own. Voila! We now had our own employee handbook. We figured the big company had probably spent tens of thousands of dollars paying lawyers and consultants to create this handbook so why not learn from them.

Over the years, we put together many updates of our handbook; eventually, we hired an attorney of our own to review the latest edition. Each time we issued a new handbook, we changed the color of the paper so we could keep each edition separate from the others.

A good employee handbook has five basic elements:

1. Administrative Policies. This section lists working hours, starting times, overtime policies, pay periods, expense reimbursement, and so forth.

2. Employee Benefits. This element sets forth and reviews the company's policies regarding paid vacation, holidays, eligibility for benefits, rules regarding sick and personal leave, payment for jury duty, medical and other insurance plan details, 401K plans, and the like. The medical, insurance, and 401K descriptions are general in nature and defer to the insurance or investment companies plan booklets regarding details of coverage.

3. *Personnel Policies.* This part of the handbook covers performance appraisals, disciplinary procedures, resignation and termination policies, severance pay policies, and complaint procedures.

4. *The Rules.* This section outlines serious and behavioral offenses with policies and penalties for each infraction. At the end of this chapter, there are two specific examples. One covers general unsatisfactory behavior (smaller sins), the other covers serious unsatisfactory behavior (big sins). Of course, these are examples only. You must consult an attorney in order to find out what kinds of infractions, discipline, and consequences are appropriate for your type of business in your state and municipality.

5. *Disclaimers.* These are here to protect you in the event that an angry former employee decides to take you to court. Include a clearly worded statement that this manual is NOT an employment contract or part of an employment contract. You should also make clear the policies set forth in the manual may be changed or amended AT ANY TIME. Insert another disclaimer stating that you are NOT providing an employee with legal rights by publishing your employee handbook. You should also insert anything else recommended by your attorney. Have your handbook reviewed by a lawyer with experience in the labor laws of your state and locality.

Have a dated receipt for each employee to sign, acknowledging they have received the new handbook. Put their signed receipt in their personnel file. Have them sign new dated receipts any time you publish a revised handbook.

A handbook can be a great defensive measure when you terminate an employee for cause and they try to come after you legally or through your state Labor Board. By having a documented rules manual and by documenting, on a case-by-case basis, how you handled the employee's unsatisfactory behavior, you will go a long way toward protecting yourself from frivolous legal actions by vengeful ex-employees. On the positive side, you can sleep better at night knowing you've treated all employees fairly and "by the book," because now you have such a book! Use Table 36.1: General Unsatisfactory Behavior and Table 36.2: Serious Unsatisfactory Behavior (p. 158) as guides to what is not acceptable and what is *really* not acceptable.

Table 36.1: General Unsatisfactory Behavior

The following types of unsatisfactory behavior may result in some form of progressive counseling/discipline, including termination:

General Unsatisfactory Behavior	Verbal Warning	Written Warning	Probation (calendar days)	Discharge
1. Use of threatening or insulting language to supervisors, fellow employees, or others on the premises.		1st Step	2nd Step (60)	3rd Step
2. Failure to record or punch, improperly recording or punching, unauthorized altering or removal of any time card or record, or permitting others to do the same.		1st Step		2nd Step
3. Insubordination or refusal or intentional failure to perform work assignment.			1st Step (90) + 2 day suspension	2nd Step
4. Wasting time or leaving the workplace without permission during working hours. Loitering or engaging in unauthorized visiting before, during or after working hours.	1st Step	2nd Step	3rd Step (30)	4th Step
5. Failure to report immediately (within the work shift) any accident on premises which results in personal injury or property damage.	1st Step	2nd Step	3rd Step (30)	4th Step
6. Violation of a safety rule or safety practice, or creating or contributing to unsafe working conditions.	1st Step	2nd Step	3rd Step (60)	4th Step
7. Failure to maintain an appropriate personal appearance, uniform, dress or personal hygiene.	1st Step	2nd Step	3rd Step (60)	4th Step
8. Failure to report to your work area after punching in.	1st Step	2nd Step	3rd Step (60)	4th Step
9. Unsatisfactory work performance. (Failure to carry out assigned duties and responsibilities in a timely manner.)	1st Step	2nd Step	3rd Step (60)	4th Step
10. Disruptive behavior and other actions which disturb a fellow employee in performance of his or her duties (slowdowns, excessive gossiping, encouraging work rule violations, etc.)	1st Step	2nd Step	3rd Step (60)	4th Step
11. Sleeping on the job and not working during shift.		1st Step	2nd Step (90)	3rd Step
12. Unexcused absences — 2 or more occurrences in 6 months.	1st Step	2nd Step	3rd Step (90)	4th Step
13. Unexcused tardiness — 3 or more occurrences in 1 month.	1st Step	2nd Step	3rd Step (60)	4th Step

Unexcused Absence An absence for any reason considered invalid by the supervisor. If an employee is absent over two days within a six month period, the supervisor may (depending on the circumstances) question the employee about whether these were justified absences. The supervisor may request documentation of future absences such as doctor's verification, accident report, etc.

Unexcused Tardiness Failure to report to work assigned within five minutes of the starting time. This includes beginning of workday and all breaks.

Multiple Violations of More Than One Work Rule Three violations of more than one work rule during a 12 month period, where the consequences for any one of the violations was a written warning will result in termination of the employee.

Table 36.2: Serious Unsatisfactory Behavior

The following types of unsatisfactory behavior are of such a serious nature that violation may result in *immediate termination* of employment.

Serious Unsatisfactory Behavior	Probation (calendar days)	Discharge
1. Any false statement made on application for employment or omission of information that might unfavorably affect your application.		1st Step
2. Theft or removal from the premises without proper authorization any property of the company or of another employee.		1st Step
3. Disobeying national, state or local laws (other than minor traffic violations).		1st Step
4. Unauthorized use or unauthorized possession of intoxicants, narcotics or other drugs on or in the company premises.	(90) discretionary	1st or 2nd Step
5. Being unfit to work due to the influence of alcohol or illegal drugs.	(90) discretionary	1st or 2nd Step
6. Willfully misusing, destroying or damaging any company property.	(90) discretionary	1st or 2nd Step
7. Fighting or attempting bodily harm to another employee.		1st Step
8. Unauthorized possession of weapons or explosives on company premises.		1st Step
9. Immoral conduct or indecency, vulgar or abusive language.		1st Step
10. Falsifying records, documents or schedules.		1st Step
11. Improper use of fire or other emergency alarm systems or equipment.		1st Step
12. Sexual harassment of any type.	1st Step (90)	2nd Step
13. Smoking inside the building.	1st Step (90)	2nd Step
14. Unexcused absence of five consecutively scheduled days will be considered voluntary termination.	1st Step (60)	1st Step

CHAPTER

37

Are You A Scrooge?
Economic Reality
for Your Employees

Too many business owners focus on hiring cheap help. Some figure they can't get good people anyway, so they go for cheap. Of course, you know that's wrong. In Chapter 32, I showed you ways to find and keep great employees. These bottom-fishing owners are always complaining about problems with employees. No wonder.

Others pay minimum wage or dangerously close to it hoping to find intelligent experts who have just a few rough edges that need to be polished. A gem in the rough, so to speak. Sometimes they find one. And, sometimes, people buy a state lottery ticket and hit the $38 million jackpot. One happens about as often as the other.

Still others have a very distorted view of what employees should cost because they have a distorted view about the cost of living. People born in 1940 remember when the minimum wage was $1 per hour. They were probably paid that if they had an after school job in high school. If their dads were making $5 per hour, they had a pretty comfortable existence. They remember when McDonalds sold burgers for $.15 and a bag of fries for $.12. A big new Ford Sunliner convertible cost less than $3,000 and a ride on the bus in any major city was $.25, and you got a free transfer. Try to get out of McDonalds today for less than $4 apiece. Bus rides cost $1.50 in most cities and some don't even give transfers.

Business owners born in the mid-'50s remember when you could buy a brand new Chevrolet Corvette for $5,500. (Corvettes cost over $40,000 now.) They recall the $2 per hour minimum wage they were paid for their afterschool job. They reminisce about the breakup of The

Beatles, too. When these folks were in high school, newly graduated engineers were paid starting salaries of $10,000. They're getting almost $50,000 now.

People born in the mid-'60s remember Rubik's cube. When they were in high school, the minimum wage was $3 per hour and a new Cadillac Seville cost $20,000. A fully-loaded Seville is now priced close to $50,000.

The point is that many business owners have lost sight of what it costs today to live at a minimum wage level. Let's face it, the minimum wage is not a sustainable wage. Today's minimum wage would have bought you a comfortable living in 1956 but it's well below poverty levels in today's dollars. It may be marginally acceptable for young people still living with their parents or older part-timers on social security and try-ing to pick up a few extra bucks. Couples and families making minimum wage struggle to keep their family together, even if husband and wife both work. They are right on the edge of eviction and homelessness. Seemingly minor things like needed car repairs or dental work will cause major problems because they live day-to-day and have no emer-gency fund. The minimum wage just doesn't cut it for most folks. Therefore, if you want to get and keep good help, you'll have to pay more. Or get very lucky.

In the early years of our plastics business, we paid poorly — right around the minimum wage level with little opportunity for advance-ment. We generally had poor employees and high turnover rates. The few good employees we got were due to sheer luck. In later years, our average paycheck was more than double the minimum wage. Our turnover dropped by a factor of four. We finally had some great employ-ees. If you want to keep your good employees, you must do two things in the area of compensation:

First, you need to set up a fair compensation system that will allow your employees to earn more than the norm for your industry or geographi-cal area. You can do this by paying a decent base wage and providing bonuses based on higher-than-normal productivity. Chapter 34 dis-cussed bonus programs. I want to emphasize that the programs I insti-tuted in my company really cost us nothing because they were entirely funded by productivity improvements made by the employees them-selves. I just wish we had started the programs sooner.

Second, you should give deserving employees raises often. Chapter 32 recommended that you review each worker's performance every six months. If employees are becoming more skilled and therefore, are now worth more, you should give them a raise and stay competitive with the job market so they won't take their skills elsewhere. A raise is a vote of confidence in your worker's future.

The minimum wage is just not a living wage, but please don't think that I'm advocating big increases in the minimum wage level. The answer is not raising the minimum wage. The real answer, to which you can respond as a business owner, is to raise the skill levels of your workers by training them and to raise their productivity levels using incentive programs. Then you can pay them a decent wage that is fully justified by their skills and productivity. You'll end up with better employees, and more profit.

Tune in to economic reality as your employees see it. Keep them satisfied and you'll keep the good ones.

The Quest
for Booger Tape

You can't keep every employee forever. Some will leave to work in non-competitive businesses. A few will either go to work for one of your competitors or go into business for him/herself and become your competitor. I've heard lots of small business owners worry aloud about this, some of them to the point of borderline paranoia. I tell them that they probably have nothing to worry about.

I can recall three instances of employees leaving to start their own plastics fabrication business and compete with me. All thought that because they knew how to fabricate and had copied down the names of some of my customers from shipping labels on outbound shipments, they could simply step in and take a lot of my business away. As you've learned so well the hard way, it's not that easy. They did the usual, predictable sales pitch, "Yuh, well, we're really good ... and we're really cheap ... and we kin do a good job fur ya. Nope, we don't got any literature yet. Nope, we don't got any customers yet. But you should try us. We're really good. Lemme send ya my business card." As far as I know none of these "competitors" are in business today.

Lenny was a pretty good employee. He was one of my production foremen. He resigned and went to work for a competitor. We were sorry to see him go. Rumor was that the competitor offered him double what I was paying and made him part of their Corporate Management Team. Hey, Lenny was good but he wasn't that good.

Allow me to digress and tell you something about the plastic display business. Many displays are made with mirrored acrylic plastic attached to acrylic, wood, or Styrofoam substrates. Now you can't use regular glue to attach acrylic mirror because the chemicals in the glue attack the mirror coating. Double-sided tape doesn't stick well. Conventional mastic adhesives don't work well either. The factories that make mirrored acrylic recommend a specific brand of gooey, rubbery tape. They don't make a big secret about it either. They'll give this information to anyone who calls and asks for it. This tape is very sticky. You can take a thin strip of this stuff and roll it up into a small ball and flick it at an object across the room and it will stick. And that's what some of our more juvenile employees used to do. Except they'd flick the little ball at another equally immature employee and yell, "Boogered ya!" And that's how it got the nickname "booger tape."

Lenny arrived at his new job and found that the first order of business was to run some mirrored displays. "How do we make it stick, Lenny," they asked. "That's easy," he replied (eager to please), "With Booger Tape!" They told Lenny to get a case of it. We heard that Lenny spent a week calling every adhesive supplier in the United States trying to order Booger brand tape. Lenny also told his new employers that we had our saws specially sharpened by Those Saw Guys in New Jersey and that we bought a special cardboard shipping container from The Box Dude in Oregon. He also tried to find The Bit People where we got our special triple fluted carbide router bits. Lenny was soon no longer part of the competitor's Corporate Management Team.

Why didn't Lenny copy down names and return addresses from our incoming shipments? As a foreman, he certainly had access to them. I think it's because Lenny was thinking like an employee not a manager or owner. Business owners seem to have a natural curiosity about things. They're snoops. They're always picking up information and filing it for possible future use. Employees generally don't think this way.

The point of my story about Lenny is that you shouldn't lose any sleep over an employee switching sides. Your customers don't just buy from you because of one employee. If you're doing a good job, they'll stay with you. Besides, you'll never know how dumb some of your employees can be until they go to work for your competitor!

Now What?

As a cook and baker, you must do something with each cake you make. Sell it. Devour it. Share it with others. Use it as a learning experience to make another, better cake. The one thing you can't do is to put it on a shelf and ignore it. If you do, it will get stale. It will become inedible, undesirable, unusable, and unsaleable.

In this section, we'll talk about your options and the future of your cake and your bakery.

CHAPTER

39

Keeping Score

Progressive, successful companies collect information. They use it to make their prosperous businesses even better. They keep score, and they don't just use financial statements as their scorecard.

The problem with conventional financial statements prepared by accountants is they are really nothing more than historical documents that have been created to satisfy the Internal Revenue Service. Unless you really dig through them, they won't tell you all of the things you really need to know to operate your business efficiently. Don't blame your accountant, though. Most accountants will stick to exactly the task you've assigned — come up with something to satisfy Uncle Sam the Tax Man.

There are three basic things you need to know about your business if you want to make it more profitable:

1. Learn What It Costs to Do Business.

I mean on a job-by-job, project-by-project, or day-by-day basis. When our plastics business was very small, John and I sought help from the Small Business Administration's SCORE program. This program offers one-to-one counseling for owners of small businesses, supplied by unpaid, volunteer mentors who are retired business owners and managers. It's an excellent program, and it's free! You can get more details about this program from your local or regional SBA office.

We were visited by our assigned SCORE representative, a genial, elderly gentleman by the name of Bernard Guthrie. Bernard had started and

165

operated several successful manufacturing businesses. He asked us to tell him about our business. We did. In our too-short relationship with him (he passed away in 1983), Mr. Gutherie had a habit of asking very simple questions that we couldn't answer properly. He never berated us. The shame and embarrassment of being unable to answer elemental questions from this wise and kindly man was enough. His first simple question was, "How much does it cost to make things?" I asked for clarification. "Well, what would you charge to make this?" he asked, pointing to a clear acrylic cube table in the corner of my office. "Fifty dollars," I replied. "How did you come up with that number so quickly?" he queried. "Well, it's easy. We use a rule of thumb. Four times the material cost. There's $12.50 in acrylic material in that cube." Taking a $50 bill out of his wallet, Bernard said, "You know, that sounds like a very reasonable price to me. I'd like to buy one of those for my living room. I think I'd like to put a lamp on top of it and run the cord through the top. Can you make me one with a hole in it for $50?" "Sure." "Good. Well, here's my 50 bucks. And, you know, I think I'd like some extra holes in it. Why don't you drill 100 half-inch holes spaced on one-inch centers on each side. Let's see. It's a five-sided cube so that would be 500 holes. OK?" We got Mr. Gutherie's point. It would have taken us many extra hours to make a drilling fixture for precise spacing and to drill that many holes. Our "rule-of-thumb" didn't account for things like that.

As a result of that meeting, we ordered a time clock and job-time cards to measure our real labor costs on specific jobs. We had one job, a very complex one, a part for a vacuum seed cleaner. We always thought of it as a very profitable job. It used less than $50 worth of acrylic and we sold it for $610. It took us a while to produce it but we intuitively felt that most of the time the components were just sitting around waiting for the glue to dry. The buyer, Jerry Noble of Noble Tree Seed Improvement Company, bought one about every two months. Whenever Jerry would come to pick up a finished cleaner assembly, he always brought an old one back with little pieces of cardboard and masking tape stuck to it with design changes and improvements which he wanted on the next one. Of course, we'd have to modify our cutting and gluing jigs to accommodate Jerry's changes.

We dutifully recorded our labor costs on the next seed cleaner we produced. We were shocked that it took 74 man-hours to make this product. That didn't include the time taken to make modifications to our jigs to accommodate Jerry's changes. Even with no profit either on material or labor, we were making all of $7 per hour on this job. Since our internal break-even shop rate was over $30 per hour, we were losing lots of money every time we made a seed cleaner.

Jerry soon stopped by to pick up his finished assembly, carrying still another cleaner with cardboard markers stuck all over it. He wanted to explain and review the new design changes. I counted 16 pieces of cardboard on it and told him that these new changes would cost $4,800 — $300 per design change. He was shocked. I explained that we were happy to be his Research and Development Department but he was going to have to fund this R&D. I also told him his new price for each one-off prototype was going to be $2,750. Now he was even more upset. I suggested that he consider a small production run of five pieces at a time. That would allow us to gain some economies of scale and that, for orders of five parts, we would reduce the unit price to $1,100 each. "But I don't know if I can sell five," he lamented. "Then maybe you don't have a market," I countered. "What about the $610 price?" "You'll never see that again," I commented, "But when you're ready to order 50 units, let's talk. We might be able to get close." He was quite distraught when he left but eventually came back with a five-piece order. We produced them and made money on them. Jerry never made any more design changes. Suddenly, the existing design had become acceptable and no further "research and development" was needed.

Earlier in this story, I mentioned the term "break-even shop rate." It is, simply, your total sales minus material purchases minus profit divided by billable employee hours. For most manufacturers, you'll get seven billable hours out of each employee on an eight-hour day. The other hour is lost because of breaks, safety meetings, shop clean-up, equipment change-overs, and so forth. You can use this concept for businesses other than manufacturing, too. Law firms, CPAs, graphic designers, contractors, and even dental offices can use this kind of job-costing system.

In case you're wondering where we got the $2,750 price for Jerry Noble, our calculation went like this:

$2,418 (74 hours x $32/hr.) + $50 material = $2,418 break-even + $332 profit = $2,750 sales price

Our break-even rate of $32 per hour was calculated this way:

Monthly sales ($16,200) minus material costs ($5,512) minus profits
(zero!) = $10,688

$10,688 is our monthly break-even point
(excluding material purchases)

During that month we had 334 billable employee shop hours.

$10,688 divided by 334 hours = $32 per hour shop rate

We measured our shop times and material usage for every job we took on. In a fairly short period of time, we developed a new method of quoting jobs, and we now could be sure that we were making a profit on every job. By being profitable on each and every job, our little company began to show a profit each and every month on the financial statements prepared by our accountant. It's like the old adage says, "If you watch the pennies, the dollars will take care of themselves."

2. Compare Financial Statements between Your Business and Published Averages.

There is a directory, called *RMA Statement Studies,* published annually by Robert Morris Associates of Philadelphia. (See Chapter 44 for more information.) This book compiles and lists data from more than 100,000 businesses. The data is sorted by four-digit SIC codes (Standard Industrial Classification). Chances are, your category of business is listed in this directory. RMA reports industry averages for selected line-item financial statement components. Here are some you should examine carefully:

a. Gross Profit

This is net sales less material, outside purchases, and direct labor costs, expressed as a percentage of net sales. If you're not making enough gross profit, you'll never make any net profit. Low gross profits are an indicator that either your selling prices are too low, you're paying too much for material, or that your employees are terribly inefficient. Low prices are the culprit 80 percent of the time. If you, however, think your material costs may be too high, contact someone who does what you do in another state outside of your trade area. Ask what they pay for materials. If it's close to what you pay, material cost isn't your problem. Your trade association can give you employee productivity numbers — like annual sales per employee. If your numbers are about average, then you can't blame productivity as the problem. Then start focusing on pricing. A manufacturing company I know well won't quote any jobs that have a gross profit below 38 percent. They say, "If we shoot for 38 percent, we'll average over 33 percent and that keeps our bottom line out of trouble."

Gross profit varies by industry. Some average industry percentages are: Graphic designers: 50 to 60 percent; Small cabinet shops: 40 percent, Glazing contractors: 30 percent; Restaurants: 58 percent; Roofing and sheet metal businesses: 26 to 27 percent; Tool and die manufacturers: 44 percent.

b. Net Profit before Taxes plus Owner's Compensation

This is also measured as a percent of sales. Some owners take large salaries and leave very little money in the business while others leave a lot in the business because they're planning some major purchases. Money left in the business varies greatly not only from company to company but, within a single business, from year to year, depending on the needs of the moment. The combination of net profit and owner's pay provides a more realistic view of the business's true profitability than net profit alone.

Percentages vary by industry. Video production companies average 16 percent. Restaurants 10 to 12 percent. I think most small businesses should shoot for percentages well over 20 percent. If yours is lower than your industry average and you're not running a fleet of Ferraris as company vehicles and holding management meetings in Tahiti, you've got another indicator your prices are too low. Most small businesses are pretty ruthless about keeping their general and administrative expenses down. The problem with the bottom line often begins at the top line.

c. Return On Total Assets (ROTA)

This is net profit before taxes as a percent of total assets. If your return is subpar, you're not working your assets hard enough. Do you have unproductive assets? Maybe you can sell them and use the proceeds to build your business. Chapter 14 discusses ROTA in detail.

d. Receivables

This is accounts receivable divided by monthly sales multiplied by 30, based on 30 calendar days in the average month. The number is expressed in days and reflects the average time taken for a bill to be paid by your customers. Is the rest of your industry or profession collecting in 41 days and you're running 55 days? You've either got deadbeat turkeys for customers or a broken collection process. Start fixing this and watch your cash flow improve.

Most companies that sell to other businesses on open account average 40 to 45 days receivables. Construction subcontractors like glaziers, roofers, and heating and air conditioning contractors run about 55 days.

One of my clients dropped his receivables by 12 days simply by calling customers and using *RMA Statement Studies* data to say, "I know you're paying my competitors faster than me and I need you to bring your payments back in line."

3. Compare Your Non-Accounting Data with Others in Your Field.

Part of our plastics business was wholesaling of plastic sheet, rod, and tubing. We belonged to a trade association called NAPD, the National Association of Plastic Distributors. (It's now known as IAPD, the International Association of Plastic Distributors.) They had a wonderful program for members called PAR (Performance Analysis Report). The cost to participate was very modest — only a few hundred dollars. You filled out a five-page questionnaire about your company and submitted it with your financial statement. The PAR folks took all of the data received and produced specific, comparative data concerning your company's performance compared to its peers. You received a report with data presented as medians, upper quartiles, and lower quartiles. Your personal copy showed how you stacked up with everyone else. Data was very specific and included non-accounting things like warehouse sales per warehouse employee, cut-piece revenue per saw person, sales per inside salesperson, gross profit by product line, sales per square foot of floor space as well as traditional measurements like ROTA, days receivable and so forth. We used this report to fix anything that looked sub-par (no pun intended). Within three years we had moved to the upper quartile of values in 80 percent of the categories reported. Those PAR reports were a great management tool for us. I recommend that you contact your trade association and see if it has a similar program. Many do.

You can also get some employee productivity information like sales per employee from trade and business magazines. American Business Journals publish weekly business newspapers in most major cities. Their publications include: *The Atlanta Business Chronicle, Crain's Chicago Business, Pittsburgh Business Times, Providence Business News* and *Las Vegas Business Times*. Based on data in their *Portland Business Journal*, I've found out small ad agencies have about $130,000 in annual sales for every employee, landscapers run about $52,000 per employee, video production companies do about $100,000 per employee, and travel agencies, $60,000. Information from printing trade magazines indicates that quick printers average $70,000 per employee.

You're not gathering data to just impress your friends, your CPA, and your banker. You need all of this information to find and fix weak spots in your business. You won't know what those weak spots are until you know what others in your industry are doing. You'll use this information to turn your business into an efficient money machine. Start collecting and analyzing numbers today. You'll never regret it.

Holy Cow!
Everything's Changing!

Someone who started a business in, say, 1947 would look back on it 25 years later and probably find that it hadn't changed all that much. Insurance agencies were run the same way. Printers were using the same machinery and technology. Machine shops had pretty much the same equipment. Looking back at 1947 from 1972 was a nice nostalgic glance at an orderly progression of change.

Not so today. Virtually every business has undergone a revolution in the last decade. And the revolution continues at an ever-increasing pace. Business owners today have seen competitors go out of business because they couldn't meet the ever-changing challenges in their business world. These upheavals have been caused by rapid technology advances, changes in our society, and new government regulations.

The technology changes are there for all of us to see. In the 1960s, computers were room-sized monsters, costing millions of dollars. They had, we used to think, unlimited power, speed and memory. Today, most laptops have more computing capacity, speed, and memory than those behemoths of a generation ago. The ability to deliver almost unlimited memory in a little box which costs far less than a new automobile has made computers suitable for a variety of mundane and not-so-mundane applications. CAD/CAM has changed tool and die making forever. Word processing programs and laser printers have, for all intents, eliminated the need for typing services. Desktop publishing has almost killed typesetting businesses. More and more insurance agencies are moving toward paperless offices with direct computer links to insurers. Sophisticated, computer-controlled engine management systems have altered the structure of the auto repair business. Cars don't need tune-ups the way they used to, so people don't patronize the local repair garage as frequently as a generation ago. The need for sophisticated diagnostic equipment has raised the price of entry into the auto repair business. If you have such a business, you need to spend a great deal of money each year just keeping your shop up-to-date.

The fax machine permits small manufacturers to do quotes for far-away customers. No longer does a customer have to visit a factory and explain what they want done. Just fax over a sketch. You'll probably get a quote faxed back to you in a day. The use of on-line services to access information and book travel arrangements is changing the face of the travel agency business. So is a slimmer commission structure offered by the airlines. A travel agency must learn to adapt — or disappear.

Changes in our society have created business opportunities and taken some away. There were no car alarm shops a generation ago. Increases in crime levels, especially car theft, have made consumers more protective of their vehicles. Sales of home security systems have skyrocketed, too.

Fifteen years ago, people loved "mall-walking" and the proliferation of shopping malls killed off many downtown shopping districts. The advice to the small retailer was, "Get in a mall or die." Many of the Mom and Pop-looking stores in malls are really multi-store giants in disguise. Things Remembered, the gift and trinket engraver, has several hundred locations. Same for the bakery, Cinnabon. Last year, a small cookie shop in our local mall was kicked out to accommodate Mrs. Fields. The mall is owned by a large company that has several malls. Keeping Mrs. Fields happy is a much higher priority than dealing with the requirements of a single location small business. Now we learn that mall traffic is declining. In 1990, U.S. consumers spent 142 hours going through malls. In 1994, they spent less than 40 hours. Part of this change is due to the growth of big box stores — Wal-Mart, OfficeMax, Price-Costco, and the like. Prices are lower and consumers will trade off a narrow selection of merchandise for lower prices. In many cities, the downtown district is returning. People want that "nostalgic" feeling. Shoppers say they have less time to shop, yet leisure time is increasing. Cynical mall tenants claim consumers are spending too many leisure hours watching television.

The television business has changed, too. A generation ago, there were three major networks with affiliates in every major metropolis and an independent station or two in each city. Today there are hundreds of cable channels. If you have a satellite dish, you can get most of them. If you have cable, you'll receive 40 or 50 of these channels. No longer do TV networks "own" the airwaves. Relatively low-cost video cameras have seemingly made everyone a TV reporter. Just as desktop publishing has revolutionized the printing business, desktop video production is changing the face of television.

The telecommunications business has changed, too. Government deregulation of telephone service in the '80s created new competition. Communications technology is evolving so fast the new phone companies have trouble keeping up. Hungry cable companies are gearing up to deal with two-way communication, something that used to be strictly phone company territory.

Consider the printing business. In the '60s, quick printing was almost unknown. Printing was a specialty trade. Most of it was single color, routine work. A print shop might decide to offer low prices by hawking 1,000 flyers for $10 or so but they'd make it up on the artwork and typesetting. They could do this because, in those days, almost no one brought camera-ready copy to their printer. The printer helped them design the piece and then typeset it, and ended up making a good profit from doing so. Printers made lots of money on routine forms, too. If the form had infrequent usage in a business, that was OK. When the business relocated in a year or so they'd have to re-order the forms, even if they had hundreds of them remaining with their old address.

Today printing is a changed market. The line between printers and copy shops is very blurry. The market is saturated. The Quick Printing Industry Public Affairs Council estimates there were 42,000 quick printers in the U.S. in 1995. Almost all are small owner-operated businesses, either independent or franchised. Many customers have desktop publishing capabilities and bring their printers camera-ready work, often on disk. These customers are far more critical of print quality. When you've created a graphic box around your text yourself and you know that it's exactly one-inch from the paper's edge, you'll be looking closely at the printed work to make sure that it isn't three-quarters of an inch, or off-center. One of my clients, who just sold her printing business said, "Customers now know just enough about printing to be dangerous." Many former users of stock forms now print their own right off their laser printers, especially if usage is low. Small businesses can buy specially designed paper stock directly from companies like Paper Direct, Queblo, and Idea Art and laser print their own tri-fold brochures, business cards, letterhead, and shipping labels. Some companies are reducing paper costs by placing their catalog offerings on a Web site instead of visiting their friendly printer to buy catalogs.

If all of this sounds frightening, you must remember that such turmoil always brings opportunities. The focus on using faxes, e-mail, and the Internet to do business has removed the personal touch. Many small businesses have begun developing a presence in their local area. They find that reaching out on a one-to-one basis gets them more business. One small printer has created a portfolio of printing success stories and idea generators that he presents at one-on-one meetings with prospects. It gets him new business and, in the troubled world of small printers, his sales and profits are on the increase.

Technological improvements present opportunities for those small business owners who invest intelligently in innovation. In the early '80s, acrylic sheet manufacturers were promoting the concept of using lower-molecular-weight acrylic to make fabricated parts. The benefit was a significantly lower materials cost. The downside was that it handled differently in processing and required special saw blades for cutting. The technology was proven; lower-molecular-weight acrylic had been used by European plastic fabricators for 30 years. American plastic fabricators are a curmudgeonly lot and grumbled about making the changes needed to accommodate this new material. Except our company. We felt the risk was low (buying a $500 saw blade, changing a few fixtures) and if it didn't work, we could go back to what we had been using. So we tried it. We liked it because it substantially lowered our costs. Within a year, we had converted 90 percent of our work to the new material. We could get more business by quoting lower prices and still keep a very respectable profit margin. We made serious inroads into our competitors' markets. Meanwhile they were still grumbling and still buying the higher-priced acrylic. It took them six more years to finally come around to our point-of-view. By then, we had taken a lot of their business. The lesson here is to jump on the innovation bandwagon as long as you are convinced the technology is proven and practical.

In the early '90s, when Congress passed the Americans with Disabilities Act, several remodeling contractors stepped forward and pronounced themselves ADA compliance experts. They could show building owners what modifications were needed to bring their structures into compliance. They had seized a business opportunity created by a change in government regulations.

I can't tell you what the future holds. I don't know how future technology will affect communications, manufacturing or services. I'm no sociologist and therefore, can only guess at societal changes and what opportunities they may bring. And who knows what the government has up its sleeve? In this chapter, I'd rather focus on the principles of dealing with change rather than the specifics. I just hope that, 30 years from now, when some budding entrepreneur (who isn't even born yet) picks up an old, dog-eared copy of this book at a garage sale laying next to an ancient Pentium-processor computer, that the principles inside this book are still relevant to his or her business.

As a small business owner, you must keep your eyes open. Changes will occur faster than ever. Upsets will happen. Challenges will appear, but opportunities will be created, too. It's your job to be alert and grab some of those opportunities for your business.

Choosing
Your Own Future

Your business is now successful. You remember the early days when every day was a struggle to survive. Those days are over. You've turned your business into a smoothly operating machine. You've delegated enough responsibilities to key employees that you don't have to be involved in every piece of day-to-day minutiae. You can leave the business for conferences and vacations. The question which keeps popping up in your mind is, "Where Do I Go From Here?" You have three basic choices — expand, coast, or sell.

In every preceding chapter of this book, I've tried to provide you with specific recommendations. I can't do that here. The path you choose is a very personal one. There are no magic formulas or rules-of-thumb. You began your business because you wanted the freedom to determine your own destiny. Your choice of paths will reflect your individual feelings, needs, and desires.

Let's examine your options:

1. Expand

There are lots of ways to expand your business. You can just keep doing what you're already doing; you can expand into new products or services; you can add locations; you can franchise your business system or license others to do what you do.

In our manufacturing business, we considered establishing a satellite manufacturing branch on the East Coast. On paper it made very good sense. We had a number of customers in the area and could probably get more if we could cut our shipping times. Our sole Oregon location meant deliveries to New Jersey took two weeks to arrive. With a plant in Pennsylvania, we could cut our shipping times to a day or two. But there were problems. Setting up another manufacturing plant would require a considerable capital investment. We were tired of being in debt and had worked hard to reduce our indebtedness over the past few years. None of our present employees wanted to relocate to the East Coast so we'd have to hire someone from the area, train them in Oregon, and send them back to run the operation. We'd be putting a lot of our assets in the hands of a relative stranger. During the start-up, we'd have to spend a lot of time traveling back and forth — a task neither my partner nor I relished. The numbers on paper looked interesting but the idea was at the outer edges of our comfort zone. We never set up the satellite operation.

One of my clients has been asked by his largest customer to set up a satellite manufacturing operation in Europe. The customer is a good, stable company and is willing to sign a contract that will cover 60 to 80 percent of the plant's initial capacity. They have provided my client with contacts at other suppliers who have already done the same thing. If my client doesn't move forward with this project, he will lose most of the customer's European business, which is considerable. My client is now in Europe, interviewing other U.S.-based small manufacturing companies to find out how they've done it and looking for other outlets in Europe for his manufactured components. If his fact-finding trip produces positive responses, he'll probably establish the new operation. He's comfortable with the concept.

You can also grow by adding new products. We manufactured plastic displays. Many of our customers also purchased displays made from other materials — metal, wood, and so forth. When questioned, several of our customers said they wished we made velvet-covered displays for jewelry. We looked into it. The manufacturing process was familiar to us and caused us no anxiety. These displays have wood or plaster substrates. Velvet material is glued to them to provide a nice, decorative finished surface. We purchased some examples of these displays and tore them apart to see how they were made. We got prices on components and began estimating the costs of producing these displays. We compared our proposed prices to current market prices. We looked very competitive except for one company who had very low prices — 50 percent below everyone else. Unfortunately, that's where most of our customers now got their displays. We asked our customers more about this supplier. They said that the company had terrible deliveries and seemed to be always teetering on the edge of bankruptcy. We asked if they would pay us 20 percent more for the same product. They said they'd pay no more than a 10 percent premium over what they were now spending. That was not enough for us to make a decent profit. We shelved this idea but reviewed it every six months to see if the supplier had folded or raised his prices. We were interested in producing velvet-covered displays only if we could make money doing so.

Greg, another client, has set up what he believes is a great system for producing and selling decorative wall murals. He is going to open a satellite store as a showcase operation. Once the idea is proven, he wants to license or franchise others. He believes this concept has potential nationwide. He is starting slowly — taking baby steps — to prove this concept. Once the concept is proven, he plans to consult with franchising and licensing experts to see if he can make additional money by having others replicate his system. If not, he'll probably just keep adding locations albeit at a slower rate.

If your business is growing and you're not comfortable with the growth you'll have to bring in managers or outside professionals to help you manage the growth. You can also stop growing and start coasting, or sell out.

2. Coasting

Many owners say they have as much business as they want and stop looking for more customers or clients. They only resume their selling and promotional efforts when needed to replace customers, clients, or patients lost by attrition. Many very successful firms choose to operate this way, especially medical and dental practices. If you have a dental practice in a growing area that provides you with a good living, freezing your size is fine. Just remember that as the area continues to grow, other dental practices will move in and take patients that might have been yours.

During my big-company days, we used to hire Ed, a one-man promotional and presentation guru, to help us with industrial trade show presentations. Ed was the maestro, orchestrating a network of subcontractors to build exhibits, make loopless audiotapes and provide visual materials. Ed loved his work and said many times, "I am the business. When you hire me, I take responsibility for getting it done — professionally and on time." Ed made a very good living because of his reputation and had as much business as he wanted to handle. He sometimes turned business away. He chose not to train another maestro. When Ed got older and tired of the business, he shut it down and retired. Ed had salted away enough earnings over the years so he could easily afford to stop working.

When you decide to coast, you must recognize that you are vulnerable to any hungry competitor. Wal-Mart has moved into many small towns where the local merchants were complacent and were coasting. Wal-Mart, which had humble beginnings as a small store in a small town, has become a formidable competitor. They have a system in place for locating an operation in a new town. Their promotional ideas are tested and proven. Their buying power is so strong they can secure merchandise at far better prices than a small retailer. It's tough for these small, complacent retailers to compete.

Many businesses stay the same for many years, making the owner lots of money. But before you coast, look at your vulnerability to market forces and competitors. Coast at your own risk.

3. Selling Out

The fact is that most business owners eventually sell their business to someone else. It's a very significant passage and it deserves its own chapter. So please turn to Chapter 42.

CHAPTER

42

Selling Out
and Getting Yours

I once knew a guy named Sid who ran a small advertising agency in Portland, Oregon. Sid's business was never very big but he had a loyal roster of clients who kept him busy and happy. As Sid got older, he downsized the agency, eventually turning it into a one-man business that he operated from his home. It continued to provide him with a good living. Eventually, Sid fell ill. He still enjoyed his little business, so he cut back on his workload by dropping a few clients and continued to run the small agency. As Sid's condition worsened, he cut back more and more, taking on what work he could and enjoying every minute of it. Sid closed his agency just before he died.

One of the benefits of owning your own business is to control your destiny. Sid did just that. There are, however, other ways to exit your business. Some businesses are family-owned and the owners work hard to create a smooth transition between one generation and the next. For most of us, the way of exiting the business is to sell it to someone else. A few make a successful public offering of stock; most sales are to other private parties or other small businesses.

Most people sell their businesses for four reasons:

The first is the opportunity to get some liquid assets. Most successful business owners find that a great deal of their personal wealth is tied up in the business. Their own fortunes are tied to the fortunes of the business. They would like to spread the risk a little by re-deploying some of their assets. Selling the business gives them the opportunity to do that. I lived on a little hill about 12 miles west of our manufacturing plant.

When I'd get up early in wintertime, I'd look eastward and see a faint red glow in the sky. I never knew whether it was the sun coming up over the Cascade Mountains or the third shift burning down my plant. This was a genuine concern for me. Our building wasn't sprinklered (because there was not enough well water to support such a system). We were dealing with flammable raw materials. If our plant had been destroyed by fire, we could have started up again in another location but it would take awhile and, meanwhile, our customers would be getting used to buying from our competitors. You can't replace $600,000 worth of finished goods inventory overnight. Our business interruption insurance would help but the problem was still out there. A fire would devastate us; it would take years to recover financially.

The second reason is a combination of exhaustion and boredom. The owner gets tired of the business. Little things begin to bother him or her. My business partner, John, occasionally had a touch of this. He would sometimes get frustrated and say, "We're successful but I'm still dealing with the same day-to-day stuff as I did 10 years ago. I hate it."

The third reason is the owner has found a new business interest and wants to devote full time to it. I met a photographer who dabbled in graphic art and now wants out of the photography business so he can devote his time to graphic design. Every day spent doing photography is a day away from his new love. He's actively looking for a buyer for the photo studio.

The fourth reason is the business has outgrown the owner. The owner had fun when the business did $400,000 per year in sales. The fact that revenues have now grown to $2,000,000 per year scares the owner. He or she doesn't want to do any more delegation, doesn't want to spend more time managing and wants to return to a simpler life. Selling this business is a good way to get the money and go start another, smaller business somewhere else.

Sometimes owners sell for a combination of these reasons.

Timing is very important in selling the business. As the graph in Figure 42.1 shows, there are four stages of a small business's life. In the start-up stage, there are no profits to speak of and, consequently, the business has little salable value to an outsider. During the growth stage, sales continue to rise, the business becomes profitable. In fact, profits are accelerating

Figure 42.1: Value of a Business at Various Stages in a Business's Life

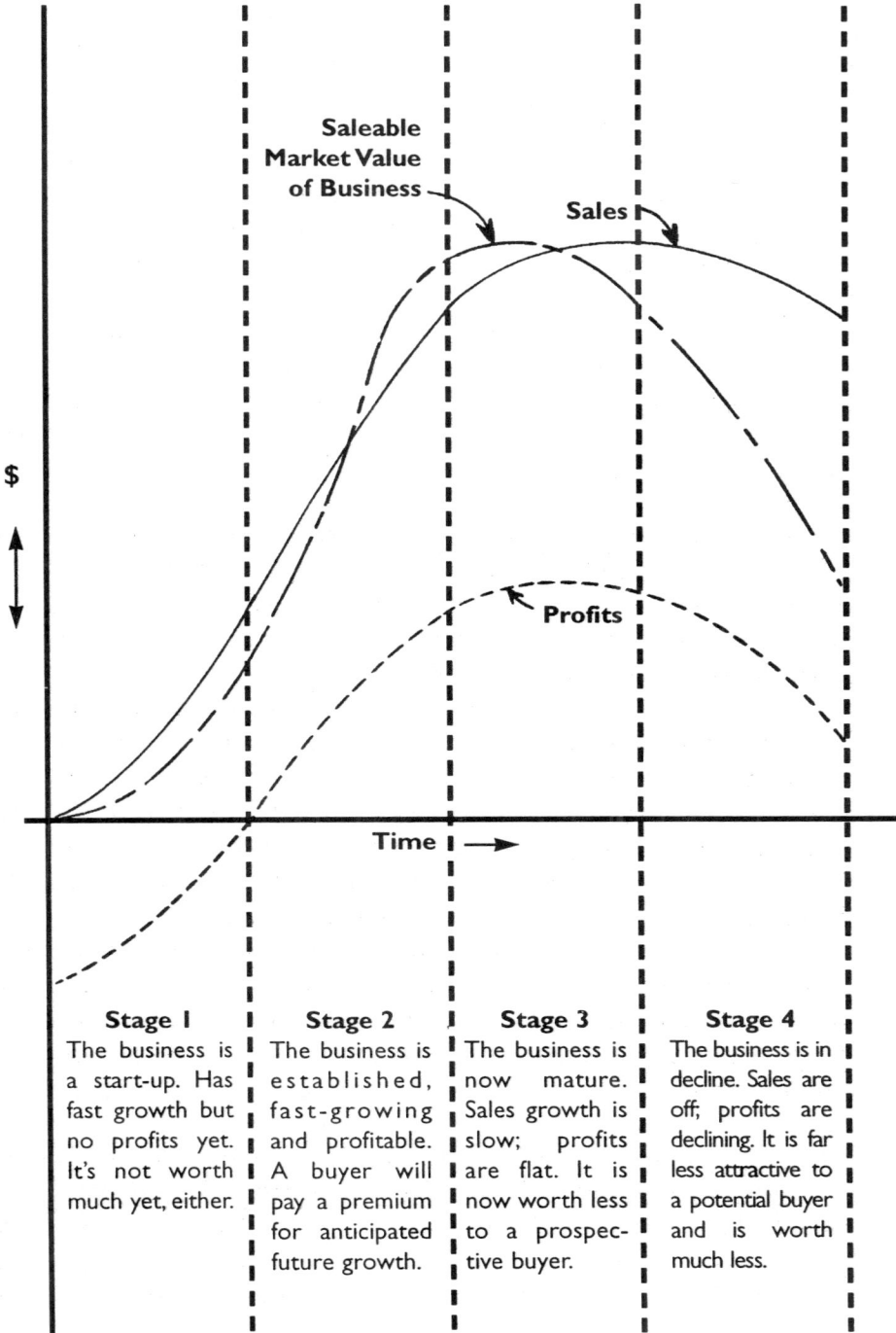

	Stage 1	Stage 2	Stage 3	Stage 4
	The business is a start-up. Has fast growth but no profits yet. It's not worth much yet, either.	The business is established, fast-growing and profitable. A buyer will pay a premium for anticipated future growth.	The business is now mature. Sales growth is slow; profits are flat. It is now worth less to a prospective buyer.	The business is in decline. Sales are off; profits are declining. It is far less attractive to a potential buyer and is worth much less.

rapidly. The business is, at this point, of considerable interest to outsiders. It looks like a money machine. Sometimes, by linearly projecting sales and earning increases into the future, the owner can convince a prospective buyer to pay a premium for the business. This is known as "selling the future." During the mature stage, sales growth slows considerably and profits flatten and may decline slightly. This brings the selling price down but the business will still command a fair price. In the declining stage, sales are flat or declining, profits are way down and the business is sold at fire-sale prices as a turnaround candidate. Obviously, the best time to sell is in the latter part of the growth stage. Happily, this is when many owners get tired or frustrated and are ready to sell.

You may think that, in the growth stage, owners who offer their business for sale are trying to palm off over-priced businesses on unsuspecting buyers. The fact is that many new buyers will continue the growth stage a long way. They bring fresh ideas and fresh capital into the business. They give it new life.

Owners always wonder what their businesses are worth. They often ask their CPAs or attorneys. While these professionals sometimes will have a rough idea of the value of a business from sales transactions they've observed with other clients, the best bet is to look to an expert. For businesses whose value is less than $500,000, a commercial business broker can give you some pretty good ideas. Interview several. Most do enough transactions that they can offer a close guesstimate based on recent sales of related businesses. For larger businesses, you need a firm specializing in large transactions. Many of these operate as business consultants specializing in mergers and acquisitions. Ask your banker for a recommendation. Many of these firms will freely offer wide-range "ballpark" numbers based on their experiences with comparable businesses. For a more exact figure, you may have to engage a business appraisal firm. Get references before you spend any money. Be cautious about business brokers and consultants, too. There are some wonderful people out there but there are also con artists. Don't just get references. Check them out, too.

What about selling to your employees? Many books have been written about the wonders of ESOPs (Employee Stock Ownership Plans). In order for them to work, you must have a motivated, stable workforce who want to be business owners. You must be willing to sell shares to them over a protracted period of time. As an owner you must be committed to sharing a lot of financial information with your workers. You must be prepared to face the fact that the employee management committee may veto the purchase of that new BMW you've wanted because they want to spend the money on equipment. Your trips to those business meetings in Maui may end, too. If those issues don't bother you, start by asking you accountant or attorney for some basic information on forming an ESOP.

Like selling a home, selling your business means establishing an asking price and being able to provide a justification for that price. You can advertise for buyers and handle the transaction yourself but I don't recommend it. You should instead consider hiring an experienced broker or acquisitions specialist. They have a much better network of potential buyer sources than you. More importantly, they can act as a "buffer" between you and the prospective purchaser. Unlike selling a home, selling a business requires many meetings, very detailed disclosures, and a lot of give-and-take. Most owners are so possessive about their business they resent the intrusion of a prospect poking around in their business and may be tempted to act undiplomatically. A good "buffer" earns his or her keep by acting as an ambassador for both sides and keeping the deal alive. For this reason, I do not recommend using your attorney as your buffer. They are often so protective of your interests they'll let minor issues become deal breakers. This almost happened to me several times during the negotiations to sell our manufacturing business. Thank goodness we had a good man by the name of Harold Murphy as our "buffer." He kept us from wrecking our deal. He made us keep our emotions in check. He sweet-talked lawyers on both sides out of unreasonable demands and conditions, keeping the deal in play. You will, however, still need your attorney to review all documents before you sign.

Deals involving the sale of a business usually have three components. The first component is a substantial, up-front down payment. This is usually paid at closing. You can ask that this money be paid into an escrow account prior to giving the buyer permission to do any due-diligence work on your business. This assures the buyer is serious and not just a tire-kicker. The second portion of the deal is often a series of regular payments over time. These are often presented in the form of consulting payments or payments not to compete. Finally, there is a balloon note to be paid to you at the end of a fixed period — between three and 10 years, depending on the business. This promissory note should be secured with a bank guarantee or with tangible real property. The exact amounts and percentages vary greatly from deal to deal, depending on the motivation of the seller and the interest and ability of the buyer. It is not unusual, however, for a deal to consist of 30 percent down, 45 percent paid over time and a 25 percent pay-off note at the end.

Some business owners think they can sell the business for cash and walk away. It rarely happens except in very low dollar-value transactions. Most buyers don't have the ready cash. They also want the prior owner to keep from competing with them. Owners can be persuaded to sign a piece of paper to that effect but buyers can enforce a non-compete agreement more effectively if some money is held back.

Most new owners want the old owner to stay on for a while until they learn the ropes. That's reasonable. You'll probably have to stay on for anywhere from a few weeks to a few months to help with the transition but my advice is to get out as soon as you can. You have run this business as a benign tyrant for a long time. You have now been deposed and paid off. A new tyrant is on board with new ideas. He or she may be deferential to you and continue to do many things which you used to do but you won't notice that. You'll notice the changes. Deep down inside you'll feel your old way was better. The longer you stay, the worse it may get for you. Get out and go do something else. Let the new owner have a free hand. If there are any more questions that require your input, you'll get a phone call.

What do you do after your business is sold? Well, I began by taking time off. It was great. It cleared my head and gave me perspective. I spent time with my family and visited with old friends. During a very cold and blustery winter, my wife and I took off for the Kona Coast of Hawaii. It was the worst vacation I've ever experienced. I woke up every morning with nothing to do. It was just like being home but with palm trees. It didn't *feel* like a vacation. That's when I knew it was time for me to go do something. So I began my quest for a new business. John Koegler, my former business partner, had a similar experience, although it took him a bit longer. John, who swore he'd never be in a manufacturing business again and would never have employees again, is now the owner of a wood furniture manufacturing business. He has employees. He loves it. Most former business owners end up owning another business of some kind or other. They get bored easily. They miss the action of wheeling and dealing with customers, employees, and vendors. They want to use their entrepreneurial skills again. Besides, they're too ornery to work for someone else!

After we sold our plastics business, both John and I (separately) started a couple of little businesses that didn't go anywhere. We kept searching and trying things until we each found businesses we now enjoy. This completes the circle because it all goes right back to Chapter 4 near the beginning of this book. Keep trying until something works!

Author's Notes

Owning your own business is a great and wonderful journey.

You will experience unforgettable moments of great drama, fun, fear, and pleasure. (Sometimes all within the same 20 minute period!)

You'll make new friends and learn more than you've ever learned in the thousands of hours you've spent in classrooms throughout your life.

You'll learn more about people from the behavior of your suppliers, your customers and clients and your employees than a psychologist learns in years of visiting the funny farm.

You'll learn more about yourself, too. You'll test your limits. You'll taste freedom as you've never known it and you'll never want to be a wage slave to another person or organization again.

It's the experience of a lifetime.

If you run your business properly, you'll attain success, wealth, understanding and the camaraderie of many business friends. You'll gain greater insight into human nature. You'll have fun. You'll feel blessed for the opportunities presented to you and you'll want to someday give the same opportunities to others. You'll become a better person than you were.

Enjoy your journey. And don't forget to enjoy your cake, too!

— Joseph M. Sherlock
Battle Ground, Washington, 1997

Resources

Reference Sources

Knowledge is power. In your quest for knowledge and data, you'll probably want to use some of these information sources. Most of these can be found in the reference section of your public library. Many of these are also available in database form on CD-ROM.

Contacts Influential or *Inside Prospects*: Published annually by Contacts Influential, Inc. Omaha, Nebraska, their business directories are produced for most major cities in the U.S. Typical listings are business name, address, phone number, relative size of business, type of business, number of employees, owner or manager of business, and whether this is a primary location, branch or satellite location. *Inside Prospects N.W.* is a similar effort by a Portland, Oregon Company called *Inside Prospects USA*. These publications are useful for finding business prospects and analyzing your competition.

Dun & Bradstreet: Offers several references, including *Dun's Business Rankings* (who's the biggest in a particular industry segment), *America's Corporate Families* (who owns what), *Million Dollar Directory* (listings and rankings of smaller, privately-owned companies). D&B also can provide, for a fee, complete reports on almost any company. Reports include hard-to-find information such as payment history, UCC filings by creditors, banking relationships, owner biographies, and, sometimes, financial statements. Since the financial information is provided by the businesses themselves, it is sometimes at the outer edge of credibility. An acquaintance once remarked, "We never actually lie to D&B, we just give them a financial statement which is two years ahead of its time."

I used D&B reports several ways. First, I always ordered a D&B report on any new prospective customer. I wanted to learn their credit and pay history. Secondly, I used them for market analysis. If I wanted to set up a new distributor in, say, Phoenix, I'd pull D&Bs on all the prospective distributors in Phoenix. Then I'd pitch the biggest/financially strongest first. The D&B report also supplied me with ownership information so I'd know who to pitch. Thirdly, I made it a practice to pull D&B reports on each of our major competitors each year. Were they growing? Were they paying their bills on time? Were they struggling? Had the old owners sold out to new people? The D&B report would tell me. D&B has offices in major cities. Their phone number is 1-800-526-0651.

Encyclopedia of Associations: Published annually by Gale Research. Lists all associations, including trade and professional associations. If you contact the associations directly, many will provide lists of association members. Trade associations can provide useful data that you can apply to your business.

RMA Annual Statement Studies: Robert Morris Associates of Philadelphia, Pennsylvania publishes an analysis of financial statements yearly. They get their raw data from banks who send customer statements with company names deleted. Lists businesses by four-digit industrial SIC code. Gives typical values like current ratio, quick ratio, sales to net worth, inventory turn, etc. for various sizes of businesses. If your library doesn't have this book, your bank will.

Rand McNally Commercial Atlas & Marketing Guide: This is a big book (18″ x 30″), published annually. Gives population and economic data on more than 128,000 U.S. locations, complete with maps. Provides market data on incomes, buying power, retail/wholesale sales data. Identifies and ranks major U.S. manufacturing sites.

Standard Periodical Directory: Published annually by Oxbridge Communications, Inc., this lists information on more than 75,000 magazines and directories published in the U.S. and Canada. Describes content, gives subscription and ad rates, provides name and address of publisher, and frequency of publication. Whenever I was interested in breaking into a new market, I got subscriptions to magazines serving that market. This gave me valuable insight into how the market worked and who the major players were. The Directory is also helpful for locating trade publications that are relevant to your business area. Oxbridge also publishes *Oxbridge Directory of Newsletters* and *The National Directory of Catalogs*.

Standard & Poors; Moodys Industrial Manual: These publications are updated frequently and provide in-depth data on companies — but only on publicly-held companies. For privately-held companies, D&B is your best bet. These reference sources are useful for evaluating customers, prospects, suppliers, and competitors who are major players in your business world.

Additional Reading

I hope that you didn't buy my book because you thought that it had all the answers to your business problems. It doesn't. No one book has all the answers — just some good ideas. In Chapter 1, I said that I read business books all the time. I still do. To continue on your road to business success, you've got to be a seeker of knowledge. Books are a great and economical source of further knowledge. So keep reading. Here's a good starter list of books for you — my personal favorites. For some, you're going to have to check the used book stores — they're out of print. Nevertheless, they're really good and worth the chase.

The Entrepreneur's Guide by Deaver Brown, Ballentine Books 1981; ISBN 0-345-29634-6. If you only read one book, read this one! The entire book is based on reality, not dreams. Deaver Brown was president and co-founder of Cross River Co., which developed and manufactured The Umbroller, the first umbrella-style folding child stroller. His book gives specific advice backed up by personal anecdotes. The chapter on finance should be memorized by all business owners; the chapter on operations is especially useful to anyone in manufacturing.

Marketing Warfare by Al Ries & Jack Trout, McGraw Hill/Plume 1986; ISBN 0-452-25861-8. The best book on marketing strategy, period. Boy, am I glad that I bought this book outright instead of paying commissions on the ideas inside. You see, I read this book three times and then followed the advice in the book and declared war on my biggest competitor. I got over $1 million in extra business in one year! Outstanding! Ries and Trout also wrote *Positioning — The Battle For Your Mind* (ISBN 0-446-30041-1) and *The 22 Immutable Laws of Marketing* (ISBN 0-88730-592-X); both are excellent books.

Guerrilla Marketing by Jay Conrad Levinson, Houghton Mifflin 1984; ISBN 0-395-38314-5. It's not really a marketing book; nevertheless, this is a very good book about advertising and promotion for companies with small budgets. Gives specific promotional techniques, too. The ideas are low-cost and can be implemented immediately. Jay has written other good books, too, including *Guerrilla Marketing Attack* and *Guerrilla Selling*.

The Entrepreneur's Manual by Richard M. White, Jr., Chilton Book Co. 1977; ISBN 0-801906454-7. This book has a lot of great ideas in it. It is obviously targeted at hi-tech, venture capitalized companies but many of the recommendations and ideas are useful to any business. I enjoyed the real-life sidebar stories scattered throughout the book.

Rene Gnam's Direct Mail Workshop by Rene Gnam, Prentice Hall 1989; ISBN 0-13-636622-8. This well-done book provides 1,014 ideas on better direct mail selling! If you have used or want to use direct mail as a way to reach prospective customers, read this book first. It has good, real-life examples in it. Rene is a recognized expert in the direct marketing field.

Dress for Success by John T. Molloy, Warner Books 1975, with later revisions; ISBN 0-446-82568-9. Excellent book on correct dress for business. Every outside salesperson should read it. Tells and shows how to dress for various types of clients. Has pictures, too, so you'll know the difference between a club tie and a regimental stripe tie. Also wrote *The Woman's Dress For Success Book* (ISBN 0-695-80810-9) and *Live For Success* (ISBN 0-553-01359-9). The men's and women's "dress" books have been updated periodically to reflect current fashions. Get the most current edition.

To Catch a Mouse Make a Noise Like a Cheese by Lewis Kornfeld, Prentice-Hall, Inc. 1983; ISBN 0-13-992914-0. Very good book on distribution and retailing; the book also has a lot of helpful information on advertising and ad agencies. Great stories, too! Kornfeld was president of Radio Shack and tells of many of the struggles they went through as they started the business.

How to Make 1,000 Mistakes in Business and Still Succeed by Harold L. Wright, The Wright Track 1990 & 1995; ISBN 0-9625588-2-6. Well-written book by a practicing small business consultant. Has actual business client stories illustrating major fundamental points about the operation of a successful small business. Like my book, Hal's is non-linear. You don't have to read Chapter 9 before you read Chapter 10. One of my clients said this is the best business book she's ever read.

The Secrets of Consulting by Gerald M. Weinberg, Dorset House 1985; ISBN 0-932633-01-3. A wonderful book which is, in my opinion, badly titled. Only consultants and consultant wanna-bes will pick it up. That's a shame because the book is about giving advice and troubleshooting problems, understanding people and more. It's about the very things you'll be doing in your business every day. Fantastic stories. I laughed, I cried, I highlighted something on almost every page. It's old but still in print because it's so good.

The Makeover Book — 101 Design Solutions for Desktop Publishing by Joe Grossman, Ventana Press 1996; ISBN 1-56604-132-5. If you have a desktop publishing program (and many of you do) and you're going to produce a newsletter (and you probably should because it's a great way to help your business grow), or set up a Web site, then this book is for you! It shows how to design a clean-looking professional document that your customers and prospects will read. The book offers "before" and "after" examples. One of my graphic artist friends said, "Desktop publishing has permitted many idiots to produce badly designed newsletters containing dull news and moronic advice in a plethora of confusing fonts all surrounded by little boxes and littered with dingbats." *The Makeover Book* won't help you with the moronic advice part but it will show you how to create good-looking documents without the dingbats.

About the Author

President of Sherlock Strategies of Vancouver, Washington, Mr. Sherlock is a graduate of St. Joseph's Preparatory School and Villanova University. He spent 12 years working for two Fortune 500 companies. He began as a mechanical engineer in Research & Development, eventually winding up as Marketing Manager for New Products. Mr. Sherlock developed new products, initiated programs to reach customers more effectively, and managed new business segments.

In 1978, he purchased a small plastics manufacturing business in Corvallis, Oregon. After 11 years, the company grew from a three-employee, storefront operation to the largest producer of acrylic store fixtures in the United States. In 1989, Mr. Sherlock sold the business to a large multi-plant wood and metal fixture manufacturer and retired. Retirement didn't last long (about as long as it took to discover what was on daytime television) and he began a second career helping other small and mid-sized businesses. As a business consultant and adviser, Mr. Sherlock has counseled and helped hundreds of clients.

Because of his real world experience in operating his own small business, he can recommend plans and programs that work. A contributor to several magazines and author of the newspaper column, "Doin' Business," Mr. Sherlock has also conducted numerous workshops on small business management and has lectured at several universities.

Mr. Sherlock resides in Battle Ground, Washington with his wife, Carol.

Index

A

Action, bias for, 10–11
Assets,
    liquid, 181–182
    return on total, 169
Attire, 99–100
Attitude, 46, 124–125

B

Bonus program, 143–148
Break-even shop rate, 167–168
Business
    coasting, 179–180
    evaluating value of your,
    177–180, 182–185
    expanding, 177–179
    selling your, 180, 181–186
    worst thing, identifying, 37–39
Business failures
    reasons for, 6–9
    statistics on, 9
Business owners,
    abscence, 151–152
    benefits of, 181–187
    benign tyrants, 152–153
    changes, 172–176

    delegating, 150
    incentives, 151
    martyr, 149–150
    morale, 150–151
    pitfalls, 149–153
    snoops, 163
Business planning, 31–32

C

Competitors, 63, 101–102
    identifying, 57–58, 60
    raising initiation fee, 84–85
    researching, 60–62, 78–79
Credit cards, 41
Customers, 129
    identifying prospective, 56–57,
    67–68, 109, 121–131, 152
    meeting needs, 53, 58–60, 73
Customer service, 94–95
    secrets of, 123–125
    timeliness, 125

D

Delivery service
    pitfalls of, 24–25
Disaster, 6
Distributors, 120

Receive $5 off any title from these related resource pages.

Enjoy and benefit from other business resources in The Successful Business Library. The following pages contain selected titles that directly relate to today's business needs. As an added benefit, you can receive a special discount by ordering directly from The Oasis Press®.

Just mention that you saw this offer in the back of *Joysticks, Blinking Lights, and Thrills* and you will receive $5 off each item that you order!

When ordering you will be asked a special code to receive your discount. **Your code is:** JOY

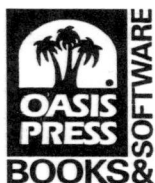

OASIS PRESS SOFTWARE BOOKS&

Empower yourself against insurance problems

The Buyer's Guide to Business Insurance is full of step-by-step guidance, ideas, and tips on how to improve your business insurance costs, coverage, and service from both insurance agencies and companies. The authors, Don Bury and Larry Heischman, bring more than 38 years of industry experience to this helpful, non-technical reference guide — showing you how to get the best property and casualty insurance coverage at the lowest prices.

Checklists, comparison charts, prepared letters, and forms make this book easy to use. If you want to save time and money through a streamlined process, and gain an unbiased viewpoint of your business insurance situation.

The Buyer's Guide to Business Insurance will:

- Help you save money and time when purchasing business insurance
- Simplify insurance purchasing with clear directions in an easy-to-use format
- Empower you with inside information about insurance people and industry methods
- Demystify the insurance process
- Eliminate confusion and complexity
- Help you avoid poor service

Be a step ahead with the accompanying software

The Insurance Assistant is a valuable tool to save you time and money. A software companion to The Buyer's Guide to Business Insurance (which is included inside the program), The Insurance Assistant will enable you to minimize insurance expenses and maximize your insurance coverage. The program guides you through the process of filling out the Underwriting Information Questionnaire, a form containing questions covering various aspects of your business. Also included are several sample letters that can be edited to meet your specific needs using the program's built-in word processor.

Binder version with no software $39.95

Paperback with no software $19.95

The Insurance Assistant Software $29.95

Binder with The Insurance Assistant $59.95

Paperback with The Insurance Assistant $39.95

SYSTEM REQUIREMENTS:
IBM compatible computer with:
- 386 or higher processor
- Windows 3.1 or later
- Hard disk with 2 MB of free space
- 4 MB RAM memory.

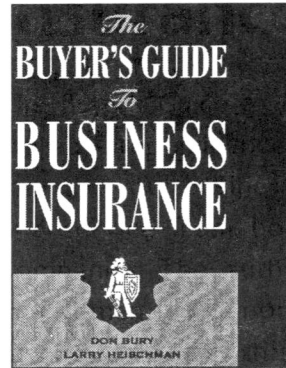

Books that save you time and money

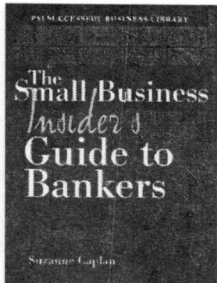

Entrepreneurs can learn how to find the best bank and banker for their business. Seven sections explain the basics: small banks versus large, finding the right loan, creating a perfect proposal, judging a business' worth, assessing loan documents, and restructuring.

The Small Business Insider's Guide to Bankers   ***Pages: 176***
Paperback: $18.95   ***ISBN: 1-55571-400-5***

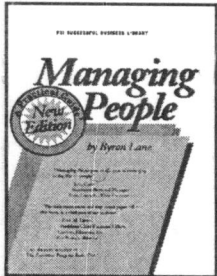

Focuses on developing the art of working with people to maximize the productivity and satisfaction of both managers and employees. Discussions, exercises and self-tests boost skills in communicating, delegating, motivating, developing teams, goal-setting, adapting to change, and coping with stress.

Managing People: A Practical Guide   ***Pages: 260***
Paperback: $21.95   ***ISBN: 1-55571-380-7***

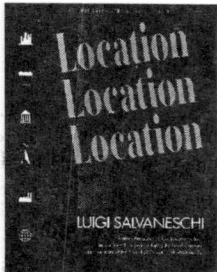

This book offers the answers to the many questions a retail business owner may have about determining the right site for a new or existing retail store. More than 80 illustrations and 12 worksheets to help you decide to rent, build, or lease at a particular site.

Location, Location, Location: How To Select the Best Site For Your Business   ***Pages: 300***
Paperback: $19.95   ***ISBN: 1-55571-376-9***

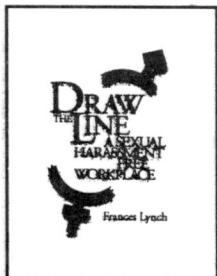

Written for managers and business owners, this book tells exactly where to draw the line on sexual harassment, and how to draw it firmly, so that employees understand and respect it. The book also clearly spells out the procedures that are most effective if a lawsuit is lodged, and gives tips on enlisting a good attorney.

Draw The Line: A Sexual Harassment-Free Workplace   ***Pages: 172***
Paperback: $17.95   ***ISBN: 1-55571-370-X***

Books that save you time and money

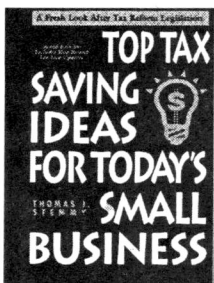

An extensive summary of every imaginable tax break that is still available in today's "reform" tax environment. This helpful resource goes beyond most tax guides on the market that focus on the tax season only, instead it provides readers with year-round strategies to lower taxes and avoid common pitfalls. Identifies a wide assortment of tax deduction, fringe benefits, and tax deferrals. Includes a simplified checklist of recent tax law changes with an emphasis on tax breaks.

Top Tax Saving Ideas for Today's Small Business   **Pages: 336**
Paperback: $16.95   **ISBN: 1-55571-379-3**

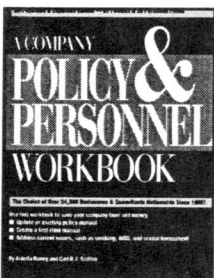

This workbook will save costly consultant or staff hours in creating effective company personnel policies. Combined into one package, you can now apply the various aspects of policies presented in the workbook to your own business' personnel framework. This helpful book & disk combination not only saves time and money, but allows you to avoid time consuming questions, misunderstandings, and legal disputes by having a comprehensive company policy.

Company Policy & Personnel Workbook Book & Disk Package   **Pages: 350**
Paperback & Disk Package: $69.95   **Runs on Windows™ 3.1 and higher**
Binder & Disk Package: $89.95

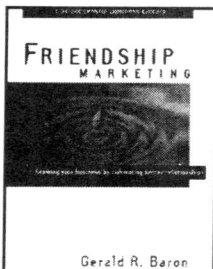

In today's cut-throat business world, businesses often disregard the importance of building lasting business relationships. This guide shows how business owners can slow down their feeding frenzy approach to business activities and build profitable and worthwhile relationships.

Friendship Marketing: Growing Your Business by Cultivating Strategic Relationships Pages: 202
Paperback: $18.95   **ISBN: 1-55571-399-8**

CompControl focuses on reducing the cost of your workers' compensation insurance, instead of accident prevention or minimizing claims. This highly regarded book will provide valuable information on payroll audits, rating bureaus, and loss-sensitive points, illustrated with case studies drawn from real businesses of all sizes.

CompControl: Secrets to Reducing Worker's Compensation Costs   **Pages: 180**
Paperback: $19.95   **ISBN: 1-55571-355-6**

Gain Valuable Feedback

THE SURVEY GENIE
EMPLOYEE EDITION

One of the most important assets any company has is its customers and employees. *The Survey Genie* will help you learn how they feel about your company and gain valuable feedback to improve your relations. It allows you to create, administer and analyze any type of survey. Available in Customer and Employee editions, both contain a database of 200 pre-developed questions to help you quickly develop a comprehensive, yet easy-to-use survey. Simply enter the information you collect and let *The Survey Genie* analyze the data and create informative reports and graphs.

The *Customer Edition* will help you learn how your customers feel about your business' advertising, after-the-sale service, customer service, organizational image, physical environment, pricing, product image, product quality and telephone service. Use this information to dramatically increase your profits, service and image.

The Survey Genie Software
Employee Edition
Price: **$149.95**

Customer Edition of **The Survey Genie** is also available. Call for more information.

MINIMUM SYSTEM REQUIREMENTS
IBM compatible computer with DOS 3.3 or higher • Hard disk with 3 MB of free space • 640 KB of free RAM memory • Graphics card

ORDER DIRECT FROM
THE OASIS PRESS®
(O R D E R   F O R M)

To order or for a complete catalog call toll free 1-800-228-2275
Mail or Fax to:
PSI Research / The Oasis Press
300 North Valley Drive
Grants Pass, OR 97526 USA
Inquiries and International Orders (541) 479-9464
FAX (541) 476-1479

Title	Binder	Paperback	Quantity	Cost
Buyer's Guide to Business Insurance w/software	☐ $59.95	☐ $39.95		
Buyer's Guide to Business Insurance (book only)	☐ $39.95	☐ $19.95		
Small Business Insider's Guide to Bankers		☐ $29.95		
Top Tax Saving Ideas for Today's Small Business		☐ $16.95		
Managing People		☐ $21.95		
Location, Location, Location		☐ $19.95		
Draw The Line		☐ $17.95		
Company Policy & Personnel Workbk w/softwre	☐ $89.95	☐ $69.95		
Friendship Marketing		☐ $18.95		
CompControl	☐ $39.95	☐ $19.95		
Survey Genie Software (Employee Edition) ☐ $149.95 (for PC Compatibles)				

If your purchase is:	Shipping within the USA:
$0 - $25	$5.00
$25.01 - $50	$6.00
$50.01 - $100	$7.00
$100.01 - $175	$9.00
$175.01 - $250	$13.00
$250.01 - $500	$18.00
$500.01 +	4% of total merchandise

SUBTOTAL

SHIPPING

$5 DISCOUNT PER ITEM

TOTAL ORDER

International or Canadian orders, please call for a quote on shipping costs.

SOLD TO: *Please give street address.*

Name:

Title:

Company:

Street Address:

City/State/Zip:

Daytime Phone:

PAYMENT INFORMATION: *Rush service is available. Call for details.*

☐ CHECK enclosed payable to PSI Research   CHARGE ☐ VISA ☐ MASTERCARD ☐ AMEX ☐ DISCOVER

Card Number: Expires:

Signature: Name on Card: